Marlene,

Hope you have a great year with English Spots!

Karen Lovett

Beneath the Surface

Karen Lovett

Plicata Press

Beneath the Surface
©2011 Karen Lovett

This book is a work of fiction. Names, characters, places, and incidents either are the product of the author's imagination or are used fictitiously. Any resemblance to actual persons, living or dead, business establishments, corporations, state or county agencies, events or locales is purely coincidental.

All rights reserved. No part of this publication may be reproduced, stored in a retrieval system or transmitted in any form or by any means, electronic, mechanical, photocopies, recording or otherwise, without the prior written consent of the author.

Cover photograph of horse and rider by Dana Pedersen.

Rider: Dannelle Haugen of Lakebay, WA.

Horse: Big Sky Darth +/ AKA Sky.

Cover photo of Joe Rein, and all other cover photos and graphics and design concept by the author, Karen Lovett.

Photo of the author by Richard A. M. Dixon

Printed in the USA on acid-free paper.

**Plicata Press**
PO Box 32
Gig Harbor, WA 98335
www.plicatapress.com

For

My friend and poet,

Gene Battell

He passed away before the printing of this publication.

## ACKNOWLEDGEMENTS

I would like to thank: Keith Bezona, Leslie Bratspis, Kristi Clark, Dick Dixon, Dawn Lawrence, Jerry Libstaff, Lance McMillan, Colleen Slater, Frank Slater, Iren Torres, Carl Tucker, Jan Walker, Carolyn Willis, Marjie Wood and members of Lakebay Writers and Key Peninsula Writers Guild for their advice, critiques and support.

Special thanks to Joe Rein, who planted the inspirational seed without which this storyline could never have been conceived.

Beneath the Surface

# Chapter 1

Sunlight filtered through the dense forest canopy as Angel's hooves beat a soothing cadence on the rutted dirt road. Carla kicked the bay's dark brown flanks, tightened her legs against Angel's sides and the horse responded, breaking from a trot to a comfortable smooth canter. Garth, a black and tan German shepherd trotted alongside. They emerged from a tall stand of Douglas fir and followed the winding path between rows and rows of six-foot tall sheared trees. After weeks of downpours intermittently broken up by overcast drizzles, the April sun was a welcome change. A veil of steam rose from the warm damp ground.

Carla relaxed in the saddle and inhaled a deep breath of evergreen perfumed air. She hummed a tuneless melody, the only human sound in the woods. The shrill cry of a circling red-tailed hawk interrupted her musing. In silence she watched the bird until it disappeared beyond tall trees, and then resumed humming.

Angel came to an abrupt halt at a bend in the road nearly pitching Carla from the saddle. Nostrils flaring, ears forward and twitching, the mare's senses focused on a rustling sound in the trees. Carla spoke in a soothing voice and rubbed her mount's neck to calm the animal before they continued.

Garth stopped, nose testing the air. Hackles rose on the dog's back and a low growl reverberated deep within his throat.

A ragged figure stepped onto the road. A fringe of brown hair extended beyond the brim of the camo cap that shielded his eyes. A grizzled beard framed his ruddy complexion, concealing his jaw line. Wide yellow logger's suspenders held up faded blue jeans. The stranger glanced in the dog's direction and extended a hand. "Good boy. He doesn't bite does he?"

Garth bared his teeth. Carla eyed the man with suspicion. "He never has."

"Jason Gerard, tree patrolman for Northwest Tree Farm." He stuck his hand into a torn pants pocket, pulled out a business card and reached up to give it to her.

Carla read his name below the company address as Angel tossed her head and pawed the ground, impatient to be off.

"Can I see your land use permit?" he asked. His mellow voice spoke with authority.

Bright light dimmed as the sun disappeared behind a puffy white cloud. A gust of wind tousled her hair. She smoothed it back with her open left hand, gripped the reins tighter in her right. She looked away avoiding his eyes, focused instead on Garth. The dog sat down, hackles lowered, mouth open, tongue lolling out, eyes intent on the man.

She looked back. "I don't have one—Carla Summers. I own Summerwind Ranch just down the road about three quarters of a mile from the south gate. Been riding here for years, never needed a permit. I know Ray Morrow, the owner. He told me I can ride on his land anytime."

Jason leaned over and held his fingers out to the dog. The shepherd moved closer, sniffed, then moved away. "We've had too many problems with illegal brush pickers and people dumping garbage, especially meth labs. I'm the only tree patrolman working for the company. They own miles of land in Kitsap, Pierce and Mason Counties. I'm spread pretty thin between Shelton and Bremerton." He looked to the right. Sunlight glinted on something that caught his attention. He walked over and picked up an empty beer can. "I've had to start coming out here more often lately. Too much trouble with trespassers." He winked and smiled.

The dog sat down, eyes and nose intent on the tangle of underbrush. Bumblebees were gathering nectar from purple-flowered self-heal growing in a patch nearby. One flew near the dog. He snapped at the insect as it buzzed off and landed on a flower close to the ground.

Jason rocked back on his heels and rubbed his neck. "Your dog's very protective of you."

"Yes. I got him when he was five weeks old and trained him myself."

"You did a good job." He turned from the dog and looked her in the eye. "You do need to pay fifty dollars and send in the permit application. Follow me, and I'll give you a form."

Jason sauntered down the road and she rode Angel behind him to an old beat up Chevy truck. Scratches and dents marred the faded red paint. The bumper was caved in. Hinges creaked as he pulled open the door. He struggled with the glove box until it finally opened, pulled out a large, manila envelope, then turned back and stood beside the horse. His eyes lingered on the full-busted front of Carla's plaid flannel shirt. Embarrassed, he jerked his head up and handed her the form. He noticed she wasn't wearing a ring.

Carla's right hand had a firm grip on the reins; she took the paper with her left, folded it and stuffed it into her shirt pocket with his card.

"If you see anyone suspicious on Northwest land, give me a call. Be careful. Some of these druggies are pretty rough guys. Wouldn't want anything to happen to you."

"Will do. Thanks for the warning." She leaned over and patted Angel on the side of her thick neck.

"See you around." His eyes followed her as she cantered away sitting straight in the saddle. Golden highlights in her brunette hair glistened in the sunlight, shoulder-length tresses blowing in the wind. The mare's long flowing black tail was carried high, dog trotting by her side. He didn't look away until she was out of sight, then started the cranky engine and headed for a favorite spot near a large beaver pond to sit and eat lunch.

He pulled up to the clearing. Tire tracks led right to the water's edge. Broken rushes and cattails marred the shallow bog and shoreline. Footprints covered the moist ground. He got out of the truck and crouched down to get a closer look at the tracks.

A large bullfrog croaked and jumped into the water creating a circle of ripples. He looked up as a pair of mallard ducks swam away and disappeared beyond the other side of a patch of reeds. A bald eagle perched high in a dead alder about a hundred feet back flapped its wings and took to the air, circled once above the beaver dam on the far side and returned to its perch. The sound of gurgling water flowing over the dam chimed in the background. Wildlife lived undisturbed in this small piece of the planet he considered his world.

Jason stared into the dank water as the ripples disappeared. A light-colored car was visible just beneath the surface. "Damn." He pulled the cell phone out of his shirt pocket and speed-dialed the sheriff's office and reported the car. "Roger that. I'll be waiting at the south gate." He drove down the road, unfastened the cable and waited.

Twenty minutes later Kitsap County Deputy Stevens pulled up, got out, and adjusted his hat. "How're you doing, Jason?"

"I'm fine, Tom, but these damned tweakers—stealing cars, stripping everything of value, dumping them, preying on honest folks . . ." Jason shook his head and frowned.

"Yeah, the creeps seem to crawl out of the woodwork. We bust 'em and try to get 'em put away, but, before you know it, they're right back out ripping people off again."

"Yep, it sucks."

"Doesn't it though? Where'd you find the car?"

"It's in a pond quite a ways back. Follow me."

Jason climbed into his truck, drove to the clearing, eased to the side and killed the engine. The deputy parked beside him and got out.

Jason pointed to the tracks he'd discovered. "I haven't been out here for several months. None of these are mine." He motioned toward the water. "Look where they go."

Stevens kneeled down and touched the ground near a track. "Guess I better call in a dive team and tow truck to pull it out. Then we'll see what we've got."

A couple of hours later, the divers stood back and watched from a distance as the aging Ford, minus license plates, was pulled out.

The divers and Stevens peered in, but murky water obscured their view. Deputy Stevens donned a pair of rubber gloves and opened the driver's door. Gagging, they stepped back; the stench of decomposing flesh permeated the air. A flood of filthy water poured out. Two bodies were slumped down in the back seat.

"Oh, my God!" Jason's eyes started to water and his nostrils were assaulted by the nauseating smell. He realized what had been at the bottom of the pond and turned aside, retching. What was left of breakfast splattered onto grass and selfheal. Over the years he'd run into numerous vehicles dumped on the miles of tree farm land spread across three counties. Stolen, stripped, dumped, none of them had bodies in them. He was totally unprepared for this.

The divers moved back. One wiped his mouth across a neoprene clad sleeve. The tow truck driver walked away puking into the brush.

*At least I'm not the only one.* Once, Jason found a dead man dumped among some trees near a main road. He smelled the rotten body long before he saw it. Expecting to find a deer hit by a car, he was shocked to discover the bloated, maggot-riddled man. He smelled the odor in his head for weeks, and nightmares haunted him long after the case was solved. The investigation had uncovered drug ties.

Local meth labs were creating a significant problem. The majority of crimes could be tied to drugs or drug money. This latest discovery brought an all too unpleasant sense of déjà vu.

Deputy Stevens held his hand across his nose, the lines creasing his forehead deepening, as he grimaced from the nauseating find. "This is a crime scene. Just leave the car," he instructed the tow truck driver.

The driver unhooked the cable. "I need a signature, then I'll be outa here. Glad I can leave." He removed a clipboard and pen from the cab of the flatbed and held them toward Stevens who scribbled his name and handed the clipboard back. The driver maneuvered the truck around and a few minutes later rumbled down the road.

The deputy brought out a roll of yellow crime scene tape and ran a strip around the car and the nearby surrounding area. Stevens said, "It'll be necessary to maintain the scene intact. I'm calling the coroner and an investigation team. Jason, go out to the gate and meet them. I don't want to compromise the evidence in this case by leaving it unattended."

"No problem." Jason was glad to get back into his truck. He brushed his sleeve across his watering eyes and drove to the main road to wait. Wind blew through the open windows, fresh air replacing the odor in the truck, but the smell in his nostrils remained.

In just under an hour, several more patrol cars, an unmarked car, van and the coroner arrived.

"Detective Jim Renfield." The stocky man wearing a blue suit approached Jason and showed his badge. "My partner, Rob Chandry." He motioned to the slightly taller slender blond dressed in a light gray suit who walked up and flashed his badge.

"Jason Gerard, tree patrolman for Northwest Tree Farm." He extended his hand.

Renfield shook his hand, "I remember you from that murder near Hidden Pond a few years back. Drug related dealings on that case."

Jason nodded. "Yeah, wouldn't be surprised if this was a similar thing. Doubt if the victims were killed on the tree farm. Criminals don't usually commit major crimes on Northwest land. They just use it as a convenient dumping ground."

Renfield looked around. "Where're we headed?"

Jason pointed up the dirt road behind him. "'Bout a mile back."

"Lead on." Renfield stopped next to the coroner's van and announced. "We'll follow this guy to the crime scene."

Jason drove off, the investigation team followed behind. He stopped before he reached the pond, pulled to the side, walked over and stood beside the crime scene tape.

The detectives parked, got out, and ducked under the tape. Renfield wiped his eyes with his arm, pulled a handkerchief out of his pocket and held it over his nose. "This's baaaadd. Thank God we don't get too many like this. I never get used to it."

With a grim expression, Chandry opened the investigation kit and pulled on a pair of latex gloves. "Me either."

Renfield donned another pair. They examined the outer surface of the car, checked for fingerprints and made plaster casts of tire tracks and footprints. He photographed the bodies and drew diagrams of the site, logged each entry into a notebook and placed yellow markers beside the footprints and tire tracks.

Chandry recorded the investigation with a video camera. The coroner examined the bodies and prepared to move them.

Renfield pointed to a weathered cigarette butt on the ground. "Jason, is that yours?"

"No, I don't smoke." Jason crinkled his face and held his nose, tried to block the pervasive acrid stench.

Renfield photographed the butt and added the location to a diagram. Chandry ran the video camera while Renfield placed another yellow marker. Renfield picked up the butt and deposited it in a labeled plastic bag, continued to examine the area and wrote more notes. "Water destroyed any fingerprints on the vehicle. Doubt there'll be any DNA evidence either."

Renfield walked over to Jason. "You never saw anything going on?"

"No, I haven't been out here since the end of January." He paused and touched his hand to his forehead. "I just thought of something. I've got a few wildlife motion sensing cameras out. Been having bear trouble. A sow and cub have been ripping up a lot of trees lately. They strip the bark off to eat the cambium layer. I'll look through the footage—see if anything shows up—I doubt the cameras are in the right location, but there's a chance."

"Check it out." Renfield turned away, eyes to the ground.

Carla, relaxed in the saddle at a comfortable canter, headed back down the road toward the south gate when Angel stopped in her tracks, then leaped sideways, snorting, nostrils flared. For the second time that day her experienced rider was nearly thrown. Garth growled, nose up, sniffing the air.

"It's okay, Angel, probably just the tree patrolman." Carla patted her trembling horse, then flicked the reins.

Angel snorted, shook her head and neck, mane flying. She turned her head, eyes wide and sidestepped. Carla entwined her fingers in the long black mane and held on with a firm grip.

"What's the matter?" Carla crooned. She kicked Angel's flanks with her boot heels, but the horse planted her feet and refused to move. *What is the problem?* She was puzzled by Angel's uncharacteristic balking. She spoke in a soothing voice to calm the horse. Finally, Angel minced forward.

A sudden thought crept into her mind. *Hope it's him. Not some creep.* They rounded a bend and saw a number of cars and men. A decaying stench replaced the fresh evergreen scent of the woods. Her eyes started to water and she raised her hand to hold her nose. Now, she understood the reason for Angel's strange behavior.

Jason was off to the side. She waved to catch his attention. "What's happened?"

He hurried in her direction, then stopped in front of the horse. "I found a car in the pond. Two bodies were in it."

A gasp escaped her lips. "Oh, how horrible! Did you know them?"

He sighed, and shook his head. "I don't know. Can't tell who they are. They've been there a while. Looks like a man and a woman, but even that's hard to see. They're still in the car. Detectives and the coroner are checking everything out."

A dark-haired man in a well-cut suit walked over and looked up at Carla. "Detective Renfield, head of the investigation team." He flashed his badge. "Ma'am, have you seen or heard anything unusual?"

She shook her head. "No . . . I haven't. Do you know when this happened?"

"No, we have two bodies in a car dumped in this pond. We don't have any information other than that right now. We'll check the missing person's lists and work on the lab results. Then we'll have more to go on." He handed her his business card. "Call if you think of anything that might help solve this crime. I'll need your name and number so I can reach you if I have any more questions."

"Certainly, Carla Summers . . ."

He logged in her name and added the address, telephone number and birthdate.

She told him a second phone number. "That's my office number. I'm an accountant in Port Orchard."

"No kidding. I never would have guessed."

She frowned, "Yeah, well . . . I clean up."

"I didn't mean to insult you. Don't forget to call if you think of anything."

"I will. If you need to reach me at work, let my secretary know what it's about. It's a small office, just the two of us."

"Thanks. Keep your eyes open. Contact me if you see anything suspicious."

"Will do. It's such a quiet, peaceful place." She uttered a deep sigh. "How could something so despicable happen here?"

"Bad things happen to good people in the best of places. Crime has no boundaries. Criminals and victims can be anywhere."

"It's so sad."

Angel tossed her head and pawed the ground, snuffling her lips with impatience.

"I've got to go." She flicked the reins and the trio trotted away passing the KOMO TV crew as they drove in.

The news crew set up their equipment and started asking questions, video cameras running. Helicopters circled overhead as news teams filmed from above. The newscaster finished with the deputies, and then held the microphone for Jason. He answered a number of questions, but he was functioning on auto-pilot. It was more like a dream than reality. He couldn't add much to what the deputies had already said, so they turned their camera back on the car.

Chandry noticed something light-colored in a salal bush and focused the video cam. "Hey Jim, look at this."

Renfield added the location to the diagram and pointed the camera. He lifted the pair of rubber gloves between his fingers. "Maybe we can get some prints off of these." He deposited them into a bag, placed a yellow marker at the location.

The bodies were removed from the vehicle and laid in body bags on gurneys. White zip-ties bound their wrists behind their backs.

The coroner leaned over the female and parted the victim's hair with a gloved hand. "Cause of death looks like a single gunshot to the head."

Renfield leaned down to get a closer look at the victim's head. "What caliber?"

"Can't tell. Not too large. No exit wound." He moved to the other body. "Same C.O.D., single gunshot—no exit. No sign of any other wounds, but it's difficult to tell with the degree of decomp. I'll know more after the autopsies. Let's get them loaded in and off to the pathologist." He zipped the body bags. Deputy Stevens helped him roll the gurneys to the van and load them in. The double metal doors slammed. Stevens wiped his eyes as the coroner got into the van.

Renfield jotted more notes. "Let me get a few more pics, then you can have them." He snapped some more pictures before the victims were loaded into the coroner's van for the trip to the morgue.

The coroner drove away and the detectives continued searching the vehicle. Mangled salal and trailing blackberries, along with reeds and lily pads from the pond, were tangled in the bumper, grill, and frame.

Chandry searched the driver's side and opened the cigarette lighter. "Find any I.D.'s over there?"

Renfield closed the glove compartment. "Nope, just a couple of used sandwich bags and a few empty soda cans. How 'bout you?"

"Nothing." Chandry closed the car doors on his side, picked up the investigation kit and carried it to the van. "I'm going to call the tow truck back out and have the car brought in."

Renfield looked at the empty license holder. *What did they do with the plates?*

Jason wandered down the road and noticed an area of broken bushes. He fought his way through the swath of trampled brush to the main road. *They drove in here to bypass the cable-gate.*

He worked his way to where the investigation team was working and called out, "Detective Renfield, I think I found something."

Renfield walked over and stood on the other side of the crime tape.

"I discovered where they drove in."

Renfield ducked under the tape. "What'd you find?"

Jason motioned to the southwest. "That direction, I'll show you." He led the way.

Chandry caught up. "Ouch." He gingerly untangled a blackberry vine from his pant leg. "I'm not dressed for this."

Jason stopped and waited. "We're almost there."

Renfield looked down at tiny burrs clinging to his suit, just back from the cleaners. "Damn."

They progressed another twenty feet. Jason stopped at the edge of the woods. "This is it." Grooves in the gravel on the roadside turned in toward them.

Renfield pushed aside a tree branch and stepped onto the crushed rock. He crouched down and ran a finger along the raised edge. "Yeah, you're right." He stood up and looked down the road.

An SUV sped in their direction, slowed as it approached, accelerated away. Three more cars and a pickup passed by while they stood there.

Chandry said, "They must have come after dark. Don't think they would have risked someone seeing them during the day."

Jason squinted in the sunlight. "It's pitch dark out here at night. Even with a full moon and clear sky you can't see a thing. No lights anywhere. They'd have to know the area really well. People dump garbage at night, but they don't drive in far. Leave it near the road, just as far as they can toss it. There aren't any houses nearby. I think they waited to make sure no one was coming and did it during the day." He looked back to the trees. "They'd be out of sight in half a minute."

Renfield nodded, "That's a possibility."

They made their way back slowly, inspecting the area, searching for clues—nothing.

Renfield wrote down Jason's contact information. "We'll have to leave this area cordoned off as part of the crime scene. An officer will be here to guard the site until we make sure we have all the evidence. You don't need to stay. We'll lock the gate when we're done. That'll keep honest people out."

"Call me anytime," Jason said, and climbed into his truck.

His mind raced as he drove home. Who were the victims? How did they end up here? No one deserves to end up like that. What were they involved in? Will the police be able to solve the crime? How long will the investigation take?

What would he do if he lost the people he loved: Becky, or Jeff? What would happen to his grandchildren? He wouldn't even want anything like this to happen to Francine, not even after all the grief she gave him through the divorce.

Carla left the tree farm and plodded along the roadside deep in thought. Did she know them? It's such a close-knit community. She knew so many locals. It is possible. She remembered Jason's warning. *Am I in danger?* She held the horse back as Angel fought to quicken her pace as they approached the turn to the familiar dirt road home.

A familiar whinny sounded as the rail fence line came into view. Angel neighed a loud response. The dapple gray, Geisha, trotted to the fence, extended her neck and head over the top rail and whinnied again. The spindly-legged black foal, Shazan, frolicked at her side.

Carla smiled at the pair and thought, *I'm so lucky*. Garth trotted across the orchard and disappeared behind a row of raspberries.

Carla walked the horse into the barn, haltered and tied her to a post. She removed the bridle, loosened the girth, and then carried the saddle and blanket to the rack. She curried the sweaty horse, combed the long black mane and tail, and then led the mare to her stall.

Angel walked straight through the stall and out the door, nuzzled Geisha, headed to a muddy area of the corral. She lay down, rolled in the mud, then got up and shook herself off. Now that all Carla's efforts were undone and the deep brown coat was covered in mud, the contented mare moved on to the water trough.

Carla watched this scene with the same frustration she always felt, knowing it was inevitable; after her careful grooming, the horse would be dirty in no time.

She headed to the house and gave a shrill whistle. Garth lifted his head and looked at her, but was reluctant to abandon the mountain beaver he was trying to dislodge from the safety of its den underground. After another whistle and a commanding call the shepherd ended his pursuit and followed her into the house.

Carla reached for one of the hand-painted flowered canisters on the kitchen counter and took out a dog biscuit. The dog, with a mouthful of teeth, removed it gently from her fingertips. He crunched it down in a few seconds, then sat in a corner of the room, his eyes following her.

She pulled the permit application and business cards from her pocket, set them on the counter, then picked up the Northwest Tree Farm card and stared at the neat black print. Jason Gerard's name, home phone and cell phone numbers were printed in small letters below the company address next to the logo—a green image of an evergreen tree.

She stuck the card under a magnet on the refrigerator door. The brown wooden horse with words, "Born to Ride, Forced to Cook," printed in white on its side, left Jason's name exposed. She put the detective's card and the form into the top drawer of her desk in her office at the far end of the house.

Back in the kitchen, Carla took a plastic bowl from the cupboard and went out to the garden to pick several varieties of lettuce, radishes, sugar peas and some herbs: lemon thyme, and rosemary. It was still early in the season; she would have to settle for a store-bought tomato. She prepared a salad, sliced some home-baked French bread and heated a bowl of homemade French onion soup with bread and Mozzarella cheese on top in the oven.

She sat down to dinner. Garth lay beside her chair, his head resting against her foot.

Jason pulled into his gravel driveway that paralleled the front fence of weathered rails. Clinging moss hid signs of rot. The small house needed paint; gray clapboards and white trim were worn in places, exposing bare wood to the elements.

Familiar loud whinnies and grumbling hungry horses interrupted his thoughts as he got out of his truck. Gravel crunched beneath his boots as he walked to the old red barn.

Ranger, his buckskin quarter horse gelding, was eighteen years old. He had an even temper and was always a pleasure to ride. Teasel, a black and white paint was troublesome, but Becky loved the mare, so he kept her in spite of her flaws. Besides, she was good company for Ranger.

He was weary from the stressful day, but he mucked out the stalls, added new shavings and put a flake of hay into each of the two hay-racks. Each horse got a scoop of grain, which they greedily ate before pulling out mouthfuls of hay.

Jason walked into the house and washed his hands. He filled a bowl with Frosted Flakes and milk, grabbed a spoon from the drawer and sat down in front of the TV to have dinner. The smell of decaying flesh was still in his nose. He lowered his spoon. His thoughts returned to the murdered couple he'd found. Who were they? What were they like? What did they do? How did they end up dead in the pond? It was all so sad . . . so senseless.

Jason dumped most of his cereal into the toilet. His stomach was still churning and the lingering odor of the corpses quelled his appetite. He tossed his soiled clothes in the laundry basket and showered, scrubbing himself with more soap than usual, willing the hot water sluicing over him to cleanse the contamination from his body and soul. He stood there until the heat dwindled and the spray ran cool. After drying himself with a towel, he searched for the remote, located it under a fold in the quilt and crawled into bed. He flipped through the channels and settled on the local news.

The murders had become a significant segment. The reporter stood at the site in front of the mud and weed encrusted car. There he was, on TV right next to the reporter with a microphone shoved in his face. He saw himself replying to questions he didn't even remember being asked.

Then a plea for information: the identities of the victims were still unknown. Anyone who might have knowledge about the crime or victims was urged to call the Kitsap County Sheriff's office. Fade out, the scene changed. It was over. The weatherman announced the next day's forecast.

He turned the TV off and closed his eyes, but sleep eluded him for much of the night. The sight and stench of the car and decaying bodies were indelibly imprinted on his mind and senses. Over and over he saw them . . . smelled them.

As he lay awake, his thoughts shifted to a more pleasant image. Like commercials interrupting a made-for-TV movie, he saw a woman whose big brown eyes looked down on him from her seat astride a bay Arabian. The sexy vision of her was the last thing he remembered before he finally drifted off to sleep.

His dreams were filled with her that night, side by side, he on Ranger; she on the bay. They galloped through fields of wildflowers, her brunette hair fluttering in the wind, golden highlights catching in the sun's rays, drawing him to her tantalizing full breasts bouncing beneath her shirt. She sat astride her mount, the snow-capped Olympic Mountains behind her. The Brothers twin peaks formed a perfect backdrop for her curvaceous body.

## Chapter 2

Jim Renfield loosened his tie. He stared at photos of the double homicide strewn across the desktop. He picked up an image of the shoeprints, studied the sole pattern, took a sip of coffee and stopped in disgust as the cold, bitter brew hit his tongue. "That's bad."

He got up and poured the coffee down the sink in the men's room. The cup rinsed, he refilled it from the machine, stirred in some powdered cream and artificial sweetener and swallowed a mouthful. "That's a little better." He returned to the desk, took his seat and thumbed through the file. He said in a loud voice, "You know how much I hate paperwork. It's all we've been doing lately. That and searching data banks on the system. Too bad those cameras out at the tree farm didn't pick up anything."

Chandry looked at him. "Yeah, that would have helped." He scratched his chin. "You know, you're letting this murder investigation get to you too much. It's taking a toll on you. You look like hell."

"Thanks a lot, Rob. You don't look so hot yourself."

"I gotta admit it's been keeping me up at night. Those sons-o'-bitches need to be taken off the street before anyone else ends up dead."

"Believe me; I'll be sleeping a whole lot better after we get the perps. Paula's been bitching about how I'm never home. Even when I'm there, my mind's on the murders."

"Me, too. Almost glad I don't have a wife to bitch about anymore."

Renfield looked at the gold-framed picture of his wife and two children. "Yeah, well, I don't envy you that. I love Paula, and I miss my kids. I feel guilty spending so much time on this investigation. It's been two weeks since the victims were pulled out of the pond. We haven't had a day off and we still don't have any leads."

Chandry raked his fingers through his blond hair. "I gotta take time to get to the barber."

Renfield felt the back of his head. "Me, too."

Sherriff Wheeler came out of his office and walked over to Renfield's desk. "How are things shaping up on the homicide investigation?"

Renfield scanned down the list on the monitor. "Both vics were killed by a single gunshot to the back of the head, execution style, hands bound behind their backs with white plastic zip-ties. The weapon, a 9mm Glock semi-automatic handgun, still not recovered. Ran ballistics through NIBIN. The National Integrated Ballistics Information Network has no weapons signature record of the gun being fired in any crimes, solved or unsolved. The rubber gloves had a good set of prints and DNA. AFIS had no match on the prints. DNA results on the cigarette butt and the gloves aren't back yet. We really need a break."

Wheeler nodded. "Don't let up."

Renfield leaned back and clasped his hands behind his head. "You'd think with all the prints in the Automated Fingerprint Identification System these guys would be in there somewhere. This can't be the first time these perps committed an offense. At least we know the victims: twenty-four-year old Timothy Sutton and twenty-six-year old Janice Williams. Didn't take long to locate their families. They were on the missing person's list. Had no ties to drugs, lived together in a rustic cabin back in the woods on the southwest corner of Kitsap County, just about three miles from the crime scene. Tim did odd jobs, mostly cutting and selling firewood while Janice was a waitress at Suds and Spuds local bar and grill on the Key Peninsula in Pierce County about five miles from their home.

Wheeler asked, "What about the families? Did you check them out? Any leads?"

"They're all clean. Can't tie any of them to the crime."

"No identification was found on either body, but Sutton's prints came up on a former DUI arrest when he was nineteen. His brother made a positive I.D. of both bodies. According to friends, 'Janice was a kindhearted young woman. She was generous and cheerful and always had a kind word to say to everyone she knew.' No one we interrogated could say why someone would want to kill her?"

Renfield scrolled down the screen and read transcripts from the interrogation of Tim Sutton's brother, Ray. "Tim wasn't the best provider, but was always willing to lend a hand to his many friends. They weren't well-off financially. Lack of education hindered his ability to get ahead in the world, but he hoped to change all that with a federal grant he just got enabling him to go to school. He was determined to turn his life around. All their plans for the future came to a sudden end. Why were they killed, if not for drugs?"

Renfield added, "A search of the couple's home turned up no clues. The dwelling had not been ransacked, and although their furnishings were meager, the place was neat. The only things missing appeared to be the car they were found in, Tim's wallet and Janice's purse. Nothing of theirs had turned up anywhere.

"There were plaster casts of footprints, a second set of tires, finger prints on the inside of the gloves, but with no suspects we've nothing to match them to. The bullets were not tied to any other crimes."

Wheeler shook his head and clicked his tongue. "Keep on it." He turned away and headed back down the hall.

Chandry walked over and leaned against Renfield's desk. "Yep, keep on it—like we haven't been working our asses off."

Renfield exhaled loudly. "Yeah—I know. Hope the DNA results will be a game changer." He sat down and rearranged the photographs of the crime scene spread before him, then rifled through the pages in the hard copy file for the umpteenth time. Photographs of Tim Sutton and Janice Williams smiled back. He had placed them there next to those of his wife and children as a reminder that these were real people who had been loved by their families and were missed. He had a duty to those families to bring closure to their ordeal and to see justice served on their behalf. He was determined the perpetrators of this crime would be caught and brought to justice.

Chandry tapped a pen on the desk top. "Maybe we ought to call up the tree farm guy. Take another look out there?"

"It couldn't hurt." Renfield searched through the Rolodex, picked up the phone and punched in the number.

"Jason, Detective Renfield here. Can you meet us? We want to take another look around."

After a brief exchange he set the phone down. "He'll be out there in half an hour. Let's go."

## Chapter 3

Jason opened the gate and waited. They didn't keep him long. After the investigators passed through, he relocked the cable and accompanied them to the pond. He watched while they searched the surrounding area.

Chandry followed the track of broken brush. "Think I'll check their entrance again."

"Me, too. Nothing else around here." Renfield followed his partner, slapped a mosquito on his neck. He accidentally swung his arm down into a thorny blackberry vine, pulled a thorn out of his hand and stretched his leg over a patch of salal. "This is a pain in the ass."

Jason followed the pair. New concrete barricades had been set into place along the property boundary to prevent anyone from driving through again. Jason said, "Everything's looking good. No one's come in here since the murders."

The detectives walked along the perimeter and studied the ground. Dried, brown leaves hung from broken reddish brown branches of salal. Renfield frowned. "Nothing. I didn't expect to find anything. Hoped maybe we missed something when we were out last time."

Chandry clicked his tongue. "Sorry we wasted your time."

Jason led the way through the brush. "Don't worry about it. Hope you find the killers. It's scary to know creeps like that are living here. I feel jumpy every time I hear the trees rustling."

Chandry said, "Can't say as I blame you. I'm sure a lot of people will feel safer once these guys are off the street."

Jason let the detectives out, but stayed behind. There was plenty of work elsewhere, but he he'd altered his work schedule, using the murders as an excuse to hang out here longer than necessary, the possibility of running into Carla, a subconscious motivation.

He walked between two rows of trees, stopped and listened. The staccato sound of hoof beats pounded on the road. He moved from between the trees, the sound got louder. His heart raced with excitement as he recognized Carla sitting straight in the saddle, one hand on the reins, the other relaxed at her side, hair blowing free in the breeze. The bay Arabian mare cantered towards him; the German shepherd followed.

She pulled on the reins when she saw him. *With all the miles of land Northwest Tree Farm owns, why'd he have to be out here again? What's the probability?* She knew there was a possibility she'd run into him, no matter how remote, but she'd dismissed it as highly unlikely. She took a chance and lost. She thought of the permit application sitting on her desk and felt guilty.

He faced her. His stocky chest filled the heavy long-sleeved work shirt. She noticed his sky blue eyes shielded beneath the bill of his camo' cap. She shifted her weight in the saddle and focused her gaze on Smokey the Bear embroidered on the front of his hat.

"Hello." Her stomach churned; she dreaded what was coming next.

"Hi. Do you have your permit with you?"

He said it pleasantly enough, without malice.

"Umm . . . Well no . . . I haven't gotten it yet." She almost choked on the words. "I intended to. I've been busy." She blinked her eyes and shifted her weight in the saddle.

He exhaled through pursed lips. "I wasn't kidding. If you want to ride on their land you have to send fifty dollars and apply for the permit. I'm not trying to be a hard-ass. After the murders, they're really touchy. I don't determine company policy. I'm just following orders, doing my job. I don't want any more trouble." Her indifference put him in a bad position.

"I'm sorry. I really didn't expect to see you. I seldom run into anyone. That's why I like coming out here. I've ridden on some of their other tracts, but this one's my favorite, besides being closest to home."

A fly landed on Angel's withers, her skin twitched. Carla leaned forward, swatted at the fly and scratched where the fly had been. "I'm sure glad I wasn't here when the criminals were. They still haven't been caught, have they?"

"Not yet. As far as I know, there aren't even any suspects. The detectives were out here a little while ago, still looking for more clues, but they didn't find anything new."

"It gives me the creeps knowing those criminals are still on the loose." She shivered in spite of the 65 degree temperature. "I don't want to be their next victim. That's a scary thought."

"Believe me, I know. I'm out here alone. I've been thinking about it a lot lately myself." He pressed his lips together and inhaled a deep breath through his nose. "What if you or I had been here when the killers were? We might have ended up in the pond too." He hadn't wanted to frighten her, but he hoped she would take him seriously and do as he asked.

A gasp escaped her lips. "What a ghastly thought. Let's hope the cops catch the culprits soon."

He asked, "Did you know the victims, Tim Sutton and Jan Williams?"

Her hand flew to her mouth. "Oh no . . . not Jan! I hadn't heard. I've been so busy at work I haven't kept up on the news. I used to see her at Suds and Spuds. Didn't know her very well. She always had a smile on her face, a real sweetheart. I'll miss her."

Jason nodded. "I liked her, too. I don't get to the Bar and Grill often, but I loved to tease her. She had the funniest laugh. I got a kick out of telling her jokes. . . . It won't be the same without her." His voice started to crack. He wiped his eyes. "Knew Tim for years. He used to park his pickup loaded with firewood for sale down in Vaughn along Elgin-Clifton Road. He was a great guy . . . my son's age." He stopped talking, bent over, rubbed his eyes again.

Carla brushed her sleeve across her cheeks wiping tears as he spoke.

Jason changed the subject. "We've put ecology blocks to make it harder for trespassers to drive in, but criminals always seem to find a way."

Carla looked away wondering if he was referring to her failure to follow the rules. "I'll make sure to send for the permit right away."

"Thanks. Make sure you do it before you come back." He rubbed her horse on the neck.

"Don't worry, I will. Sorry I didn't do it before. I just didn't think it was a big deal."

"I know. If it was up to me, I'd let you ride anytime without one." He grinned and winked.

She shrugged her shoulders. "That's okay. I know you're just following orders."

The horse shook her head and snorted.

"I need to get going. Angel gets impatient."

"All right, but make sure you have your permit next time."

"I said I would. I promise." She turned and rode off, her horse's head high and the dog running by her side.

Jason watched her until she was out of sight. He hadn't meant to sound so gruff.

How much danger were they really in? He wanted to believe they were safe, but with the murders still unsolved, were they? He hoped so.

His thoughts turned to Carla and he regretted having so little time to talk to her. He hoped he'd see her again. She didn't seem to want to spend much time talking to him.

Francine left him so many years ago. He hadn't been with many women since then, just that unfortunate brief time with Arlene. After that, he'd immersed himself in work.

He vowed, if he ran into Carla again, he wouldn't let her slip away so easily.

\* \* \*

Three weeks later, Jason stopped in at the neighborhood convenience store in Vaughn. The store on Highway 302 on the Key Peninsula in Pierce County was just a few miles from his house. He was surprised to see the front window boarded up.

"We were burglarized a couple of nights ago," the store clerk explained. "Thieves broke in sometime during the night after we closed. We turned surveillance tapes over to the sheriff's office. The burglars stole lottery tickets and cigarettes. The cops should be able to catch them. If they try to cash in the lottery tickets we'll get them."

"Hope they find 'em, soon." Jason paid for his gas, bought some chicken, JoJos and a soda. He shook his head as he walked out the door.

"Hey Jason, how's life treating ya?" A familiar voice greeted him.

"Not too bad, Dave. How 'bout you?"

"Some scumbag stole my excavator a few months ago. I parked it out on a job right in town. It was gone in the morning, trailer and all. Can you believe it? Makes it damn hard to earn a living. I'm still haggling with the insurance company."

"That sucks. What are they going to do with it? Can't expect to take it out on the road without getting caught."

"You wouldn't think so, but after three months seems like someone would have seen it. Hope they didn't chop it up for the metal or parts. Damned tweakers would sell their mothers for a few bucks for drugs. If only the scrap metal dealers would wise up and quit buying from these guys. They're just in it for themselves, too. They don't care about us poor honest working folks trying to stay ahead."

Jason tugged the bill of his cap. "I know what you mean. You heard about the bodies I found out on Northwest Tree Farm?"

"Yeah, saw you on the news." Dave slapped his thigh and exhaled loudly. "That was really something."

"It's sure kept me awake nights."

"I'll bet. Let me know if you hear anything about my excavator. It's a Kubota—with a thumb on the bucket. My company name, 'Winthrop Construction,' is painted on the cab."

"Will do," Jason nodded. "What's this world coming to?" He stowed his bag of groceries, turned the key in the ignition and drove away.

## Chapter 4

Renfield sat at his desk massaging his aching temples. The files of the Sutton/Williams murder case were neatly stacked in a pile. No new leads had come in and the case was wearing him down. There were still no matches to either the fingerprints or the DNA sample. Sleep eluded him. He'd lie awake for hours trying to think of something he might have missed; still no solution in sight.

Lack of sleep was taking a toll. His usual topnotch appearance with sparkling brown eyes and infectious cheer were absent. Dull, sunken bloodshot eyes peered out from puffy bags of skin. His dark brown hair was lifeless. He slumped in his chair, stared at the phone. As if on command it rang. Startled, he jerked up and bumped his knee on the edge of the desk.

"No kidding?" His heart pounded; he rubbed his knee. "What great news. We'll be right over." He hung up the phone, his tight-fisted arm shot up and he let out a cheer. "Yes!"

Mouths open, everyone stared in his direction as he announced, "We've got a match on the fingerprints. A burglary suspect was arrested in a convenience store break-in on the Key Peninsula. His prints match the prints from the gloves found near the car. The dumb shit stole a bunch of lotto tickets and was stupid enough to try and redeem one. They busted his ass for the burglary and he's locked up in the Pierce County jail." He pulled on his blue blazer and adjusted his burgundy tie. "Ready to go, Rob?"

"You bet!" His partner grabbed his jacket and headed for the door just a step behind Renfield. "Finally, a break in the case; there's a light at the end of the tunnel."

They took the steps two at a time in their rush to the car. Renfield whistled an unrecognizable tune as he drove to Tacoma. The wheels of the squad car rumbled across the grate onto the new Narrows Bridge. "Traffic's not too bad today; that's a good sign. Maybe things will turn around for us now."

Chandry looked over the side at the choppy blue water several hundred feet below. "Hope I'm not on this thing if a big earthquake hits."

"It's supposed to be earthquake proof."

"Yeah, right."

They crossed the grate on the east end of the bridge and took the Pearl Street exit and headed up 6th toward the Pierce County jail. Fifteen minutes later, they were searching for a parking place. After driving around a second time, Chandry pointed and said, "There's a car pulling out."

Renfield pulled in as a gold SUV coming from the other direction sped up trying to beat them to the spot. "Ha, don't think I'm going to let you take our space."

They walked into the lobby of the Pierce County jail and spoke to the receptionist, who examined their photo IDs and badges.

"Jim Renfield and my partner Rob Chandry. Detectives from Kitsap County here to question one of your prisoners, Michael Freeman."

The receptionist typed the name and looked at her computer screen. She removed her glasses and looked at Renfield. "You'll need to speak to the designated officer. He'll arrange to have the prisoner brought up for interrogation. I'll call his office and have him come down to meet you."

While they waited, Chandry leaned his back against the wall, his fingers tapping the hard surface. Renfield paced back and forth in the hall, the thudding of his shoes out of sync with Chandry's fingers.

"You're gonna wear a path in the floor," Chandry said.

"Naw, my feet would wear out first. It can't be too much longer anyway."

He was right. A tall, burly uniformed man approached and adjusted the belt beneath his noticeable paunch. "I'm Officer Mason. You're here to interrogate one of our inmates, Michael Freeman?"

"That's correct. We have reason to believe he's involved in a double homicide in Kitsap County. Was a DNA sample taken from him?"

"No. We didn't need one. You'll have to do that yourself. He's waiting in the interrogation room. This guy's dumber than a box of rocks. I don't know if he's linked to your investigation."

"We'll check him out. Did you get a search warrant?" Chandry asked.

"Yes, but you'll want to get another one to cover your case," Mason said.

Renfield said, "We'll need to get a copy of the interrogation video."

"That's no problem. We'll download the cam into the computer and burn a disk before you leave."

Renfield and Chandry stopped to lock their guns in a safe before they were led to the interrogation room. A guard unlocked the door and let them in. A scruffy, square-faced man with stringy blond shoulder length hair was seated at the other side of a table. His orange jail-issue jumpsuit hung loosely on his scrawny frame. The deep-lined face appeared much older than his twenty-four years.

"I'm Detective Renfield, from Kitsap County." He took the seat opposite the prisoner, removed a recorder from his pocket and turned it on. "This is my partner, Robert Chandry." He gestured toward Rob, who leaned casually against the wall behind him. "You've already been read your Miranda Rights; they still apply. We have fingerprints tying you to a double homicide in Kitsap County."

Narrow cracked lips opened wide. "Whoa. I ain't sayin' nothin' without a lawyer." He raised his cuffed hands in front of his face.

"Okay, you can have one brought in, but we're gonna nail you. If you co-operate and let us know who else was involved, we could make it easier."

"I ain't got nothin' to say."

Renfield looked Freeman in the eye. "If you say so. It's up to you. We can prosecute you for two counts of murder one. We're going for the death penalty. You take some time and think about it."

The prisoner bit his lip; his fingers dug into his thighs.

Chandry offered, "How about a cup of coffee?"

Freeman shifted blue eyes toward the smiling face. "Yeah."

Chandry knocked on the door and the guard let him out. He spoke to the guard, then returned with a Styrofoam cup and set it in front of the prisoner. "Here you go."

"How do you know Tim Sutton and Janice Williams?" Renfield asked.

"Don't know 'em." Freeman picked up the cup. He took a sip then chewed the Styrofoam rim.

Renfield raised an eyebrow. "Really? That's interesting, because we found your fingerprints near the bodies."

"You're lyin'. I ain't been near 'em." He downed the rest of the coffee and crushed the cup.

"You're done with that?" Renfield nodded toward the flattened Styrofoam.

"Yeah." He threw it towards a garbage can. It hit the rim and bounced off onto the floor.

Chandry knocked on the door. He told the guard. "You can take this guy away."

The guard came in, took the prisoner by the arm and pulled him up. "Come on; time to go back to your cell."

Renfield called out after the prisoner, "We're not done with you. We'll be back to continue our conversation." He turned off the recorder and stuffed it in the pocket of his blazer.

A fleeting look of panic crossed Michael Freeman's face. He glanced over his shoulder as the guard led him out.

Renfield took a pair of latex gloves and a plastic bag out of an evidence collection kit. He donned the gloves before picking up Freeman's discarded cup, placed it in the bag, and sealed it. "Let's get this back to the lab. We'll see if this matches the cigarette butt."

They waited for the camera to down load. Renfield took the DVD and the cup in the evidence kit with them and locked them in the trunk.

"We need to search his house as soon as possible." Renfield was already figuring out how soon he could get the warrants. "We'll go in with the team from Pierce County, but we need to be able to search for any evidence that'll tie in to our homicide investigation. I want to make sure we're covered no matter what. I don't want to risk having any evidence thrown out on a technicality by some dumb ass attorney. As soon as we get back, I'll take care of the paperwork."

Chandry said, "I'll start a rush on the lab results. Think we got him where we want him."

## Chapter 5

The four red laced Wyandots clucked noisily when they saw Carla. They followed her from the other side of the chicken wire until she disappeared behind the hen house. Black and orange wings flapped as the hens charged up the ramp. They pushed and pecked each other fighting for position at the feeder. Carla watched and laughed as she scooped in grain. She peeked in the nests looking for eggs, but it was still too early. Garth pranced at her side; the sun barely rose above the treetops as she walked the fifty feet to the horse barn.

The horses whinnied as soon as they saw her coming. By the time she opened the sliding door, they were all nickering in their stalls. She filled the hay racks and fed them grain and noticed there wasn't much left in the bottom of the barrel. She needed to make a run to the feed store and decided to go after breakfast. As she walked out, she could hear munching until she closed the sliding door behind her.

Back in her kitchen, she gave Garth a scoop of dog food, put the kettle on for tea and made an omelet. The water boiled, she poured a cup of tea and sat down to eat. Jason Gerard entered her thoughts as she lifted the cup to her lips. She paused, then she took a sip.

She'd gotten her permit a few days after she last saw Jason. Although she had ridden on Northwest Tree Farm land almost every weekend, and sometimes after work, she hadn't run into him. She wondered if he was helping the detectives with the murder investigation.

After cleaning the kitchen, she drove her pick-up truck to the feed store and couldn't stop thinking about him.

Something about him struck a chord with her. She couldn't put her finger on it—but he was different—nothing like any of the sophisticated men she'd been involved with. There was a rugged quality about him that intrigued her.

Jason turned the key in the ignition of his truck. The engine ground and sputtered, but didn't start. *Come on.* He tried again. This time it caught and chugged roughly for a minute before it settled down and ran somewhat smoother. He gave it a little more gas and started down the road.

He pulled into the feed store lot, parked and set the brake. Inside, his eyes shifted toward the counter, drawn by the recognition of those sun-kissed locks. He'd seen that same head of hair almost every night- in his dreams. He'd spent countless hours running his fingers through those silky tresses and caressing her warm, soft body. Somehow, he suppressed his emotions and approached her.

"Hello," he said, trying to sound casual.

She turned, looked at him, seemed to focus on the fringe of hair visible beneath the rim of his baseball cap.

"Did you get your permit?" he asked.

"Yes, it came weeks ago." Her voice sounded sharper than she intended.

"I'm glad to hear that."

She was wearing a pair of tennis shoes instead of riding boots and her legs were sheathed in a pair of tight fitting blue jeans. He hadn't realized how tall she was. He'd never seen her off her horse. With her feet on the floor, she was just slightly taller than his five feet eight inches. A sky blue tee-shirt with a gray Arabian on the front drew his eyes. She filled out the shirt so the horse's head had a lot of dimension, the outline of her breasts stretching the fabric.

Jason caught himself staring, and averted his gaze. He couldn't seem to keep his roaming eyes away. He reached up and tugged his hat brim to shield his eyes, and stuffed his hands in the pockets of his jeans.

"Ma'am, have you finished your order?" The girl behind the counter asked.

Carla jerked around. "Yes, I'm sorry. That'll be all."

The clerk gave her the bill and Carla ran her debit card through the machine. She took the receipt and turned to Jason. "I'll wait out in the parking lot so we can talk after they load my feed."

"I'll be right out." He grinned.

"I'll pull my truck up out of the way and wait for you."

He watched her walk away, eyes on her swaying hips.

As soon as his pickup was loaded, Jason drove over and parked next to Carla. He got out, walked over and stood beside her open window. His fingers twisted the fabric of his jeans. "Have you been riding much?" He stuck his hands in his pockets to conceal his nervous fingers.

"Yes, several times a week. I wondered where you were." She smiled at him.

"I've been very busy. There's no shortage of work."

She laid her fingers on the edge of the door. "Do you ever take a day off?"

"Yeah, I've been thinking I really ought to do that more often. Are you doing anything tomorrow?"

"Riding."

"How would you feel about having some company? I have horses, too. I could meet you at the same entrance you use. I live less than a mile from there."

"That would be nice. How about meeting at nine? I'll pack a lunch."

"Great! See you then."

Jason plucked his keys out of his pocket and strode back to his truck. He got in, sat back and closed his eyes, inhaled a deep breath and exhaled slowly. After a few more deep breaths, his heart rate felt normal.

He couldn't believe his luck running into her. Carla had been on his mind ever since he first laid eyes on her. He was pretty gun-shy when it came to women, didn't want any more bad experiences. He didn't think his heart could take it, not to mention his finances. Breakup-ups were costly, both emotionally and financially. But he was lonely. He missed companionship. Every time he saw an elderly couple walking hand in hand he wished he could have that kind of lasting relationship. Living alone was not a choice he preferred, it was just something he'd grown to accept. He looked forward to the next day.

Carla decided to skip riding that day. After the feed was unloaded, she got busy in the kitchen, measured out ingredients and started the bread machine, then baked a batch of cookies. While the cookies cooled on racks, she went out to the barn and mucked out stalls. Finished with that job, she ran her fingers across her saddle, and thought about going to work on her tack. She loved the scent and feel of clean leather. It added something special to riding to have everything in good order.

Instead, she decided to spend some time tending the garden. The sun was out, weather pleasant, a perfect day to be outside. Working with plants and soil was therapeutic. Her mind could wander aimlessly while her hands and fingers kept busy. Her arms were strong and tanned, an added benefit. She took pride in the fruits of her labor.

She pulled on her gloves, then kneeled on a pad in the northwest corner, yanked weeds in a bed of lettuce: green leaf, bib, red and green romaine, red oak leaf, arugula. After that, she progressed south to rows of broccoli, Swiss chard, kale and brussel sprouts. She tossed weeds into a green garden cart and heard a hen cackle in the henhouse. *There's one egg.* She stopped and stood up. Three other chickens were gathered in the pen, clucking, their eyes following her.

"All right." She pushed the cart out to the chicken pen, opened the wire door and threw in the weeds. "Here you go, girls." The three birds made a mad dash for the pile and picked at the fresh greens. The hen who'd laid the egg, peeked out, saw the others scratching at the new delicacies and ran to join them. Carla laughed as she watched. They were more entertaining than TV.

Garth kept watch between diversions for whatever critter caught his attention. His patrolling was one of the reasons her garden and nearby orchard were so successful. He kept the rabbits, mountain beavers and deer away. Deer repellents didn't seem to do much good; she'd tried them all. Without him, Bambi would descend on vulnerable plants like a plague of locusts. She faced that problem after her last dog died. Garth took care of the situation without any coaching.

She hadn't rushed to get another puppy. The heartbreak of losing Shelby could still bring tears to her eyes. Her faithful companion of fifteen years had died of cancer four years ago. She'd gone a year with no dog, but after battling deer and constantly losing, she finally made the decision to get another.

Her heart melted the instant her eyes set on the small black and tan puppy at the kennel. He licked her face with his pink tongue, and she was his. His happy, exuberant personality reminded her of her favorite country western singer, Garth Brooks. So he became Garth.

She rolled the empty cart to the next row and started in on the carrots. Her mind drifted to Jason as she worked. He seemed to be interested in her. Why? Was he just concerned for her safety? She finished the carrots and continued into a dense bed of green leafy spinach. A slimy path led to a half-eaten leaf. *Dammit.* She lifted the leaf, uncovered a two-inch long brown slug. She picked up a foot long sharp pointed stick kept for the purpose and pierced the slimy body. She scraped the curled, dying slug into the cart, stood up and made another trip to the chicken pen.

She moved on to the peas, working along the fence line careful to keep from damaging the closely planted stems. Thin tendrils wrapped around the green, plastic-coated weld-wire, securing the sugar peas to the support. She moved around the inside northwest corner and continued for thirty feet to the east side, then stopped, stood up, pressed her hands against her lower back and stretched. "Uoohhh."

She looked at the four rows of foot tall corn, radishes, beets, garlic, onions, beans and tomatoes. She wiped her arm across her sweaty brow. *That's enough for today.*

She fed the last cartload of weeds to the chickens, gathered the eggs, picked enough greens for a salad and then went inside for lunch. Garth followed her. She gave him a biscuit and he settled at her feet while she ate a salad and sandwich with a glass of lemonade.

She looked down at the dog. He licked her hand. Dogs were such good companions, content to please, always happy no matter what. A little food or a pat on the head and they were a friends for life.

Still, she never gave up hope of finding a man to share her life, but so far the best males in her life had all been dogs. She'd lost her optimism and became increasingly leery from one relationship to the next, so it was with a degree of skepticism that she prepared herself for the next day's ride.

Carla woke up long before the alarm went off at 5:30. She showered and dressed, fed the chickens and horses, and packed their lunch by 7:15. To get Angel ready, she brushed down the mare, saddled and bridled her, then put lunch into a saddle bag.

She looked over at the dog lying a few feet away. "Garth, what do you think? Am I making a mistake?"

He turned his head, eyed her and whined in response, then came over and licked her hand.

She knew he couldn't understand, but he was a "talkative" dog and she was comfortable sharing her thoughts with him. She enjoyed listening to his canine responses. "Let's go," she said as she mounted her horse and trotted down the driveway, Garth, as always, at her side. They reached the gate at 8:30. She dismounted and sat down on a rock, picking handfuls of grass, feeding them to Angel while they waited for Jason. Garth lay down near her feet.

She didn't have to wait long. A few minutes later, the mare's ears flicked forward and she let out a whinny; an unfamiliar, deeper whinny replied. Garth leaped to his feet.

Jason turned into the path next to the gate. The two horses touched noses, and then Jason's horse stepped back, snorting at their first encounter.

"Good morning," Carla said, and gave him a smile.

"Good morning. Have, you been waiting long?" He hoped not. He had expected to be the first one there and was surprised to see her waiting for him. Glancing at his watch, he noticed it was still only 8:40. Always very punctual, he was often frustrated by lateness of others. Francine was never on time. He was pleased. It was a good start.

Carla looked up at the large brimmed, dark leather western hat covering the top of his head. An improvement over the baseball cap, but she wondered what the top of his head looked like. She stood up, placed her foot into the stirrup, and was astride her horse.

Jason looked up. A few small white puffy clouds floated across the pale blue sky. The sun was still low in the sky and the air relatively cool. They were several hours from the warmth of midday. "It's a glorious day for a ride." He hadn't ridden in years, but he had looked forward to this more than he'd anticipated anything in a long while. He couldn't even remember the last time he took a day off from work. His job kept him occupied and took his mind off the state of his personal life that was in shambles.

He entered the tree farm first, taking the path around the cable gate. Garth was right behind him, followed closely by Carla on Angel.

They ambled along silently, side by side, continuing the slow pace. Periodic snuffling of the horses punctuated the rhythmic cadence of hooves on the hard ground while a chorus of birds serenaded them. A hint of breeze rustled the trees.

They rounded a bend in the road and came to the pond where Jason had discovered the car containing the bodies. That memory forever tarnished the image of this peaceful place in his thoughts. Once a haven, a refuge from whatever problems he sought to forget, it had become a reminder of the worst in human nature. Still, it drew him here as a magnet to iron.

"Let's stop for a while," he said and dismounted.

He held the reins and looked up as she slid off gracefully. Her firm, well-rounded jeans caught his attention and briefly took his mind off the murders.

As she turned to face him, his eyes went to her breasts that filled out the fine-textured turquoise shirt. He forced himself to look up to her face, unmarred by make-up, dark brown eyes with the long, thick lashes, and full red lips. He suppressed the urge to take her in his arms.

Instead, he asked her to hold his reins while he gathered some nearby wild flowers, yellow buttercups and white daisies. He cast them into the pond, and then stood in silence. A minute passed before he turned back and took the reins.

"Those poor people, what a terrible tragedy," she murmured.

"Yeah, I don't think they were murdered here, but since this is where the bodies were dumped, there are negative vibes here now." He looked at the dried tire tracks and the many footprints still evident—grim reminders of the violent, abrupt end to the lives of two people who touched his life and to whom he felt a permanent personal attachment. He felt a strange common bond with them.

They were human beings with mothers and fathers, brothers and sisters. They had loved, and were still loved and missed by their families and friends. How could someone have so little regard for other human beings? It was unconscionable, unimaginable, and so permanent. He turned away and remounted. She followed suit.

They continued past the pond and wound their way along the road between rows and rows of trees until they came to the end of the section. They rode around the cable, crossed an arterial, then took the path around the next gate. They'd been heading up a rise, and came out to a clearing on a plateau overlooking the whole area. The Olympic Mountains stood in all their glory in full view: Mt. Constellation, Mt. Walker and The Brothers. Snow still blanketed the high peaks and contrasted sharply with the blue of the sky. This side of hood Canal, Green Mountain and Gold Mountain were barely visible above the treeline. Bumble bees and butterflies flitted between abundant wildflowers: lavender and blue lupine, pink wild rose, white daisies, yellow buttercups and here and there a spotted orange tiger lily.

Carla took a deep breath, as though tasting the evergreen scented air that filled her lungs, broke the silence. "It's beautiful here. How about some lunch?"

"I'm ready. This is a great spot. We can sit on that log over there." He nodded towards an old downed fir.

They dismounted and tied their horses to nearby trees. Carla brought their meal to where Jason was sitting, handed him a bottle of water and a sandwich. She sat down a couple of feet away. Garth lay at her feet, eyes intent on his owner, but still watchful of Jason.

They ate in silence for a few minutes before Jason said, "This is a great sandwich. The bread is really good. I usually just throw a couple of pieces of white bread together with some meat in the middle."

"That's not very healthy. If you're going to take the time to eat, it should be something you enjoy. I make my own bread. I know what's in it and it tastes much better."

"I'm always so busy; I never have much time to worry about food."

They discussed his job on the tree farm, her work as an accountant, their homes and horses—nothing with emotional complications.

Carla noticed he'd finished his sandwich, "Would you like some cookies?"

"Did you bake them?"

"Yes." She held out a plastic container.

He reached in, picked one out and took a bite. "Chocolate chip—my favorite."

They finished the rest of their lunch in silence, Jason delighted in the splendor of the surroundings enveloping them in peace and tranquility. It was the main reason he loved his job.

Being in the company of this woman brought him to a higher level of euphoria. Her laughter, like bells, awakened a part of him he thought was lost forever.

Carla watched him close his eyes and turn his face to the sun toward the sun. She allowed her mind to wander. She loved this place though she'd been there countless times. It never got old. She was grateful to have space like this and have the time to enjoy it.

Being on horseback, meandering through the countryside was therapeutic. Problems evaporated into the pure evergreen-scented air with the soothing flow of motion and rhythmic cadence of hooves accompanied by an avian serenade. The contrast of bright snow-capped mountains against blue sky, varied textures, shapes and colors of wildflowers and green trees added visual pleasure to create a total sensory experience. There was nothing like it. Somehow, it served as a substitute for the emotional fulfillment her life lacked.

She always reveled in it, but it had become a solitary pastime. Other than her horse and dog, she didn't have another companion to share the experience. Being with Jason added an unfamiliar dimension that changed it all, and in some ways, made it even nicer.

Memories of Randy returned—the pleasure of spending time with someone. Many years had passed before she had finally been able to compartmentalize those thoughts into a secluded portion of her brain. It was as if she had excised those ancient wounds and laid them to rest at last. Now, they rose to the surface, unnerving her. Those niggling thoughts she had fought to suppress alarmed and confused her.

She had control of her life and was content. Men brought too many problems. Issues she didn't want to deal with. She didn't need a relationship. This had been a nice change of pace, but she wouldn't see him again.

The shrill call of a red-tailed hawk caught their attention, brought them out of their reverie. They watched as the bird circled above the clearing, harassed by a few persistent starlings. The birds disappeared beyond a wall of tall fir.

A damp nose on her hand brought her back to the moment. Garth was impatient and eager to be back on the road. A glance toward the horses told her they were content to rest. Their eyes were closed and each had shifted up one hind leg.

Carla hated to break the spell, but interrupted the silence. "I guess it's time to head back. I've got chores to do."

"Yeah, I've got things to do, too. It's been such a pleasant day. I hate to see it end."

"It has been really good, hasn't it?" She stretched out her long legs and touched her toes.

He dared to ask, "What do you think about doing this again next week?"

"Yes, I'd really like that." Carla couldn't believe the words came out of her mouth.

"Then it's a date."

On that note, they rose from the log. She gathered up the remains of their lunch and replaced them in the saddlebag. They untied the horses and were soon remounted, returning the way they had come. Arriving back at the gate, they paused.

"What do you think about meeting next Saturday? Same time, same place?" he said.

"Sure. That'll be great. Bye." Carla turned Angel and headed toward home.

"I'll see you then." Jason called out.

She felt his eyes watch her ride off. She sat straight in the saddle, appearing confident, in control.

Carla wanted to beat herself over the head. She looked at Garth. "What was I thinking? What an idiot. I already decided not to see him again. How could I be so stupid? Well, it's not like it's really a date. He's just a riding companion."

Angel's ears flicked around in response to the words she couldn't understand. The anguished tone of voice was unfamiliar.

## Chapter 6

Renfield and Chandry were on their way to Collier's place to join the police search. They passed the tree farm where the bodies were discovered and continued south down the road a couple of miles. The blacktop was slightly rougher as they left Kitsap and entered Pierce County. The car swerved to miss a chipmunk that darted in front of them.

Chandry grabbed the dash. "Jeeze, we need to get there in one piece."

Renfield grinned. "We will. Didn't want to see the little guy smeared on the road. It's only another couple of miles. Should be on the right." He slowed and turned down a gravel road.

Chandry pointed at the address. "That's it."

Official cars lined the long, meandering driveway of the expansive old farm on the northwest corner of Pierce County. A thick line of fir, alder, big leaf maple, dogwood, madrona, hazelnuts and a dense tangle of undergrowth concealed the house from the main road. Moss and lichen clung to gnarled limbs in an aging orchard near the house, filtering light in an intricate lacework pattern.

Renfield parked behind a line of law enforcement vehicles, beside a Pierce County Sherriff's van. "This place is only about four miles south of where the bodies were dumped."

At eight in the morning, uniformed deputies, plain-clothed detectives and members of the SWAT team surrounded the

Collier farm, guns drawn, prepared for the worst. Renfield and Chandry crouched behind the patrol car.

Renfield said, "Let the SWAT team move forward. Stay back here till we know it's safe." He inhaled the sweet fragrance of lilac wafting on the gentle breeze from a tree about ten feet away. Bumble bees and bright colored butterflies flitted on long cones of lavender blooms.

Police spread out over the entire area like ants on an anthill. They were closing in. A brindle pit-bull barked menacingly as they came around the side of the yellow two-story clapboard house. The dog held back and watched them warily, tail tucked between his legs as the men moved forward.

Numerous outbuildings and dilapidated sheds marred the landscape out back. Cars, trucks, heavy equipment, machinery, travel trailers and motor homes, in various states of disrepair were jammed between the buildings.

Half a dozen black and white barred rock hens fled into an unpainted, weather beaten chicken house. They huddled together and peered out at the invasion of unfamiliar men.

Someone called out, "Better call the humane society and get someone out here. They're going to have to come and pick up all these animals."

The SWAT team, guns drawn, fanned out around the house. Five members moved cautiously beneath a cascading arbor of red climbing blaze roses. A pair of yellow and pink bicolor peace rose bushes overhung both sides of the steps leading up to the front porch. Their aroma filled the air.

Three men proceeded with caution to the front door flanked on either side by another officer. The leader rang the doorbell—no answer. "Kitsap County Sherriff! Open the Door!" They rang again, tried the knob, prepared to break in.

The door creaked open. An elderly silver-haired woman in an electric wheelchair faced them, inhaled a long loud gasp from an oxygen line to her nostrils. Mouth open, eyes bulging, her chest heaved as she exhaled. The clear line dangled from her chest, trailed across the foyer and continued out of sight. Creases in her forehead and face deepened. At last she said, "Who are you?"

"Kitsap County Sheriff, Ma'am. We have a search warrant for these premises." They pointed to their badges, held out the warrant.

"What for? I've done nothing wrong."

The burly six foot five officer looked down. "What's your name?"

"Nora Collier." She looked up directly into his eyes.

He stood beside her, motioned the other to search the rest of the house. His voice softened slightly. "Do you live alone?"

"No—my son Greg lives with me. He's my caregiver."

"Anyone else staying here?"

She turned her head. "He's got friends living out back."

"Is Michael Freeman one of those friends?"

"You mean Mick? Yes, he lives in a trailer behind the house."

"What do they do out there?"

"Auto repair. Got a shop my husband Frank built." Her thin-skinned hand pointed to a picture on the wall. A smiling middle-aged man held a huge salmon by the gills. "He died—four years ago." She ran her tongue around cracked lips. "I need a drink."

She maneuvered her wheel chair into the kitchen, grabbed a bottle of water out of the refrigerator. Hands shaking, she struggled with the cap, spilled some on the stained beige and pink square-patterned vinyl floor. The bottle pressed to her lips, she swallowed a mouthful. Water dribbled between several missing teeth and ran down the front of her pink sweatshirt. She took another drink, capped the bottle and set it on the lace-covered oak table next to a green cut-glass vase filled with fresh flowers, lilacs and peace rose.

"Do you know the names of his friends?"

"Only a few, he doesn't bring them in." She sucked in and exhaled a few more deep breaths. "You can see. I don't get out much."

"Does he discuss his business?"

"No, it's none of my affair. As long as they don't bother me, I don't care. I got enough to do just breathing and living." Swollen, arthritic fingers worked the scraggly hair of her long braid. "I spend most of the time in my room. I don't have energy anymore, and I just don't feel good enough to do much. Greg takes care of me."

"Do you have any other family?" The officer looked around the cluttered room, eyes searching for clues.

"My daughters don't live here. One lives in Seattle, the other's in San Francisco. They're good women, got nice husbands and kids." She pointed to more pictures hanging on the wall, smiled narrowly. "My grandchildren."

"You better call them. We're going to search the house and every inch of this property."

"What for? I told you; we haven't done anything wrong."

"We'll see about that." Several more members of the SWAT team walked past her and moved through the house room by room. "All clear!" They worked their way back, continued outside. Renfield and Chandry and some uniformed deputies took over the in-house search.

The deputy heard the sound of drawers being pulled out and the contents dumped.

Nora started to roll across the room. "Ooohhh, don't go messing with my stuff! I told you . . ." her voice trailed off as she gasped for breath.

Renfield said, "We better get someone from social services down here to assist Mrs. Collier. I don't think it's safe to leave her on her own. I'm calling right now."

While they sifted through everything in the house, the majority of the force concentrated on the outbuildings. The

SWAT team led the way, guns drawn, each group focused on a different entrance to the buildings, trailers, and motor homes.

A blue pit pull joined by the first one they'd seen came from behind a tin-roofed building. Barking and snarling, blue lunged at a deputy. Someone fired a gun. The dog yelped, fell to the side, silenced. Its companion ran back behind the building.

"Hated to do that." The officer who fired wiped his eyes. "I like dogs."

"You had no choice. Glad you did. Not sure I would have had time." His chest heaved, he looked away, brushed a sleeve across his cheek and he turned back. "You saved me." He thumped his partner on the shoulder. "Thanks man."

A deputy knocked loudly on a trailer door. "Kitsap County Sheriff, Open up!"

No one came to the door. Another officer broke out a window and threw in a flash-bang grenade. Half a dozen more stood back, guns drawn. A small dog barked from inside.

Moments after the explosion, a bearded, longed-haired man dressed in Tee-shirt and boxer shorts bolted out, choking and rubbing his eyes. Smoke billowed around him in the open doorway. "What the hell!" He bent over, coughing.

A uniformed deputy grabbed his arms, and fastened his wrists together behind him with flex cuffs.

A tan Chihuahua came to the door, sneezed and followed the man, turned to face the deputy, barking, snarling; tiny gnashing teeth grabbed the deputy's pant leg and tore a hole.
The deputy shook his leg, brushed off the dog. "Dammit"

A young woman wearing a thread-bare, frayed flannel nightgown staggered out carrying a wailing toddler in her arms. She saw the dog land in a heap on the ground. "Chico!" The dog rushed to her side as she set the child down, and the two of them collapsed in the dirt, gasping between sobs. The barking dog backed against the woman's leg.

"Why are you doing this to us?" the mother shrieked.

"We have a search warrant for everything on these premises." A deputy grabbed her and restrained her wrists behind her, tightening the flex cuff till it bit into her flesh.

"Ouch! You're hurting me! It's too tight!"

The little boy, wearing only a diaper, clung to her side, his tiny fists twisted tightly in her gown. The two of them shivered in the cold. The trembling dog whined, teeth bared.

"Mommmmyyyyy! Mommmyyyyyy!"

Her man was pulled aside, and a deputy told him his rights as he led the suspect to a waiting patrol car, pushed him down onto the back seat and closed the door.

After the smoke cleared from the trailer, a couple of deputies entered to search. A uniformed woman remained near the mother and child huddled together shivering in the cold.

"I'm sorry he made that so tight."

She put another cuff on the woman's wrists and cut off the first one. "That should be a little better."

"It's so cold out here. My little boy needs clothes and a coat."

"I'll see what I can do." She walked up to the door of the trailer and called in, "Hey, would one of you bring out some clothes and a coat for the little boy?"

A few minutes later a deputy came to the door holding some of the child's clothes. "Here." He handed them to the deputy guarding the mother.

"I can't get him dressed without my hands," the woman said.

"I'll cut the tie off so you can get your son dressed, but I'll have to put another one on when you're done."

The child's mother dressed her son with the officer's gun trained on her. When she finished, her wrists were fastened behind her as before.

A dozen officers stood back from the door of a large, sagging wooden shop with a rusty, corrugated-metal roof. "Kitsap County Sheriff. Come out with your hands up."

Nothing happened. A deputy turned the knob, and then a shot rang out, splintering wood as it tore through the weathered door. A flash-bang grenade and two canisters of teargas were lobbed inside after two more shots were fired.

A couple of minutes passed with nothing happening, and then a gravelly voice called from inside, "Were comin' out!"

"Toss your weapons out! Hands in the air!"

A bearded, 6 foot-plus, bear of a man came to the door rubbing his eyes.

"Throw down your guns!"

He tossed a handgun aside.

"Get your hands in the air!" A SWAT team member commanded as several of them trained their rifles on the suspect.

Another man, shorter and thinner, hands in the air, followed behind the first. "I ain't got a gun!"

"Down on the ground!" a deputy ordered.

Both men lay in the dirt. Their wrists were handcuffed behind their backs. Several deputies surrounded each man.

A deputy yelled at the large man, "What's your name?"

"Greg Collier."

An officer leaned down and grabbed Collier by a ham-sized bicep. "Come on. Get up."

The two suspects were yanked to their feet and marched to waiting cars.

A deputy recited, "You have the right to remain silent . . ."

A total of seven men and two women were rousted out and arrested. Four children were taken into protective custody to be turned over to Child Protective Services.

Every inch of the house was searched. It came up clean, but other buildings revealed numerous illegal activities.

After suspects were rounded up, the detectives searched the remaining outbuildings. "Hey Jim, look at this: ammonia, match sticks, packs of Sudafed. They were into drugs big time." Chandry read off the list as he took notes.

Renfield shook his head, appalled at the enormity of the operation. "We're going to have to get the Hazmat team out here. They were cooking up a lot of meth. This is just the tip of the iceberg."

A deputy came in and reported, "The largest building is full of car parts—a chop shop. We ran the VIN numbers on the vehicles; most of them are stolen. Some of the cars outside are totally trashed. Everything of value was stripped out before they were demolished. There's even a stolen excavator, the one taken in Port Orchard a couple of months ago."

Deputy Stevens said, "I wonder what they were doing with that. I figured it was chopped up for scrap."

Renfield picked up Collier's Glock, inserted it into an evidence bag and handed it to his partner. He was pondering the magnitude of the operation. "These guys were into everything, a full blown crime operation. A good portion of criminal activity in the area must be centered here. This raid ought to put a dent in some of it. They must have been able to operate for so long without detection because the farm is isolated and most of the stuff was inside buildings."

Another deputy reported, "The team found a large field of marijuana growing way out back in a clearing near the woods. There's a trailer full of mail—identity theft—big time. We found lottery tickets from the convenience store burglary and a large stockpile of weapons. These guys caused no end of grief."

Renfield wiped a greasy smudge off his hand with a handkerchief. "I'm sure these guys murdered our vics. We need to make the connection." Knowledge that they finally had the suspects brought a sense of relief that was tempered by the volume of work left to do.

Chandry looked to the far side of the grounds and saw the dead dog lying in a pool of blood on the ground. "When's Pierce County Humane Society going to get here? It's safe now. They need to do something about these animals." He followed Renfield to a clearing behind the buildings and was stunned by the amount of evidence being bagged.

Renfield said, "Sifting through all this stuff is going to take time. We need to be on the lookout for anything that might tie into the homicide investigation." He walked over to a fifty by twenty bare patch of ground. "Looks like they were going to put in a garden.

A long piece of metal was stuck in the dirt. Chandry reached down and pulled on the rusty steel, but it remained firmly stuck in the ground. "I'm sure there must be something here. It's just a matter of locating it in the midst of all this other stuff."

Renfield was confident the Sutton/Williams case would be solved, but he was uncertain how long it would take. "There's such a mountain of evidence against these people, it's like looking for a needle in a haystack. I'm sure these are our guys. We're talking a lot of man hours. The crime lab's going to be busy for some time, that's for sure."

Chandry stared at a pile of tires. "This operation must have been going on for years. I don't know how these guys eluded us for so long."

Renfield said, "It was just a lucky break we got them now. One stupid stunt by one of their guys with no brains, and he takes down the whole shebang. I bet his cohorts wish they'd thrown him into the pond with the other two." He couldn't suppress a grin when he thought about Michael Freeman's attempt to cash in on the stolen lottery ticket.

Chandry leaned against the excavator. "Dave Winthrop is going to be real pleased to get this baby back."

"Yeah, we don't know how the two murder victims play into this. We've still got no motive, but the pieces of the puzzle are here. We just have to figure out how they fit together." Renfield handed Collier's bagged gun to Chandry.

Chandry took the gun, "Let's get it back to the lab and run the ballistics tests."

Renfield leaned back against a building and loosened his tie. "I want to get a crack at our suspects. We may be able to get some of these people to rat out the killers. They aren't going to want to take a fall. If we can get someone to talk, that would sure be a break. We'll just have to wait and see." He looked out over the Olympics. "The sun's going down. I'm ready to call it a day. We'll leave the site well-guarded, and come back in the morning. Truckloads of this stuff have gone off to be logged in as evidence already."

He started to walk back to their car. "Okay everybody; let's call it a day. Time to put this to bed. We'll be back here again in the morning, eight o'clock sharp. Go home and get a good night's sleep."

"Jim, I don't know about you, but I feel like a load has been lifted off my shoulders. I know we have a lot of work to do, but at least now we have something to work with."

"Yeah, I know what you mean. I'm going home, put my feet up and relax with a beer. It'll be great to sleep for a change. I'm sure Paula will be relieved to have me home in a reasonable frame of mind. We'll be able to attack this thing with renewed energy tomorrow. I want our suspects to stew in a cell for a while before we question them."

When the deputies drove up to guard the site for the night, Renfield went over a few details with them before he and Chandry got into their car to leave.

# Chapter 7

Saturday morning Carla woke at 5:00, showered, fed the horses, ate breakfast and made lunch. Soon, she was on Angel, deep in thought, clip-clopping down the road, Garth at their side. Jason seemed nice, and she could tell he liked her, but she couldn't trust her heart to make the right choices. She needed to keep her head together.

Some women had good luck with the opposite sex, but it certainly hadn't happened to her. She was content to have a male friend, but as for pursuing a romantic relationship with Jason, she didn't want to put herself through that again. No matter how nice men seemed at first, things always ended badly. Jason seemed busy with work and his life, so perhaps he would be content to keep things at a platonic level.

Carla heard a whinny ring out, and Angel replied before Carla saw them. It was only 8:30, a half-hour early, but Jason was already there.

She waved, and when she saw the smile flash upon Jason's face, she put negative thoughts aside, determined to enjoy the day. "How do you feel about picking up the pace today? I'll race you to the pond." She kicked the mare's flanks.

The horse sped off, her hooves digging into the soft ground as she left the pair behind. Garth bolted after them. Jason followed suit. The big quarter horse was unaccustomed to having another horse in front. His long strides ate up the ground, and he passed Angel running flat out. Ranger reached the pond first, but only a few seconds ahead of the mare. She was a little smaller, but well-muscled and spirited.

The riders stopped to give the horses a chance to recover after the exertion. Garth flopped down on the ground, tongue lolling out, panting rapidly. Jason had nearly lost his hat; he readjusted it on his head.

Horses breathing normally again, they proceeded down the road. Faster than their last trip, they entered the next section, cantered past the log they'd stopped at the week before, and kept on going. Northwest Tree Farm owned many tracts of land. Riders could leave one, enter another and continue on for miles. They paused before crossing the arterial, and entered the section on the other side.

They came to another pond after a brisk trot. Jason pulled up. "Feel like taking a break?" He hoped she was; his thighs and back were aching. *His* body needed one. He was glad it was a week since their last ride. Unlike Carla, who was obviously in good shape, used to riding often, he had been stiff and sore after last week, and it had taken him several days to recover. He wasn't willing to admit that.

"Sure, I think the horses could use one." Carla raised her right leg across the saddle and slid to the ground with ease, looked at his horse and saw the buckskin gelding was breathing heavily, sides heaving, his coat damp. "Your horse hasn't been ridden much." She noticed Jason, bent over, taking deep breaths, walked Angel to the water's edge and flashed Jason a grin. "He looks out of shape."

Jason tried to stifle a groan as he dismounted and led his horse to the pond where Angel was already drinking. A group of water striders skimmed away across the surface as Garth plunged into the pool, taking long drinks as he splashed. Cool, soaking wet, and no longer thirsty, the big dog bounded out and shook himself, flinging water all over Carla and Jason. They ran back laughing, trying to get out of the way. It was a warm day and they knew they would dry off.

Jason rubbed his sore butt with his hand. "This is a good spot for a picnic."

Garth ran through the brush around the pond, then flopped down and rolled until he finally came to rest on his side. Legs stretched and tongue lolling out; he looked like he was smiling.

Carla inhaled a deep breath through her nostrils. "What a fantastic aroma. I'm glad Garth found mint to roll in instead of a dead animal," she said with a chuckle.

Jason smiled back. "You have the most wonderful laugh—sounds like wind chimes."

Carla put her hands on her hips, her expression looked doubtful, "Really—I don't know. No one's ever told me that before." She reached down, picked some mint, crushed it between her fingers and sniffed her hands. "Mmmm, I do love it here. Let's sit by the water."

Jason pointed at the ground. A tiny green tree frog hopped across the moss toward the water. "Almost squished the little guy."

"Thank goodness he was quicker than you." She grinned and handed him a paper bag.

They ate sandwiches and cookies and sipped bottles of water. Jason sat facing her; he wanted to watch her. *She has the cutest dimples when she smiles.* After waiting all week to see her, he was content.

A pair of mallards flew down, wings out-stretched as they splashed into the pond. An unseen Flicker called nearby. Large iridescent dragonflies darted above the water like tiny helicopters among tree reflections on the surface.

Carla swallowed a bite of sandwich. "Do you have any family, Jason?"

"Yes. My parents still live in West Seattle in the house where I grew up. My brother's in Kalispell, Montana and I have a sister in Cordova, Alaska. My son, Jeff, is an electrical engineer, works for the utility company in Tacoma and my daughter, Becky, is an elementary school teacher in Everett. I'm very proud of them, but I don't get a chance to see them often. I worked hard to pay for their college tuition. It was important to me since I never went myself. Wish I'd lived with them all the years they were growing up. I missed that, but I was there for them when they needed me."

"What happened with your wife?"

He looked away and watched the ducks on the pond and then looked back into her eyes. "Francine—well, we just sort of grew apart. We got married young, right out of high school. I joined the Army. We lived in different locations, Germany, Oklahoma, New York. I got sent to the Middle East—Iraq and Afghanistan. Eventually, we ended up back here in Washington. We just sort of grew apart over the years. We're still friends. Things just didn't work out. Guess I never really understood why."

"How long were you and Francine married?"

A sad look crossed his face. "Twelve years." Jason finished his sandwich. "How 'bout you? Were you ever married?"

"I was . . . twice. My first husband, Randy, got into drugs back when we were still in college. We got married after we graduated. We used to do everything together: Skiing, scuba diving, farming, raising animals. He had a great sense of humor. We used to laugh a lot. We had so much fun. My dad used to call him 'that funny guy'. He was my best friend and the love of my life. But he got really screwed up and just kept getting worse. I didn't do drugs, and couldn't deal with it any more. We fought all the time. I could never understand it—he chose drugs and his druggie friends over me."

She sighed and stared into the water. Her fingertips dug into the moss. At last she spoke. "We divorced after three years. He ended up married to a young woman who dropped out of high school, another druggie. I heard they had a child, and then got divorced, but I haven't seen him in eight years. It took a long time for me to recover from him. In some ways, I never did. It affected all the relationships that came later. He broke my heart. I never found anyone else like Randy."

Jason reached over and laid his hand over Carla's. His fingers traced hers. She did not pull away and he was encouraged. He sensed she wasn't ready for anything more, so he contented himself with this limited contact. "Jeeze . . . I never did drugs. Haven't had much experience with people who have, except, of course, for the trouble they cause out here in the woods. I've always avoided having relationships with anyone who did."

"Believe me, you don't want to; it ruins lives. I can't imagine why so many people start. It's so expensive. Druggies lie and steal to support their habits." Her facial expression became grim. She leaned forward and ran her hands through her hair. "I never found one positive thing about it."

He finished his sandwich and took a drink of water. "I dated a woman for a year—Arlene. She was an alcoholic." He groaned and rubbed his legs. "That was bad enough."

"After what I went through, I hate everything about drug users."

"That's understandable. What about your second husband?"

"Walter . . . we were married four years; I don't know how. I loved him, but I didn't like him very much. It was more a physical attraction, I suppose. We had nothing in common and didn't do anything together. A marriage like that can only last so long. After we were married he became verbally abusive. That escalated to physical abuse; he became just plain mean." She shrugged her shoulders. "Uhhhnn—I don't know why I tried to stick it out."

He raised his eyebrows, his voice sounded puzzled. "Why would you stay with someone like that? You're so smart, well-educated. You support yourself very well. You could do so much better."

"I know. I know." She looked away, eyes cast down at the ground. "Somehow, I thought he'd change, he was so apologetic afterwards. I allowed him to destroy my self-esteem. I guess I was just feeling like such a loser after all that. He pretty much turned me off to men. I've gotten used to being on my own. I've adapted quite well actually."

He reached down, plucked a clover leaf, and twirled the stem between his fingertips. "Do you have any kids?"

"No. I wanted to, but in the midst of all those problems, it was just never the right time. Now it's too late."

"Did you have any other relationships after Walter?"

"Oh—I tried a few times, but I've come to the conclusion I'm a magnet for dysfunctional men. I've run into some real losers." Her lips pressed together in a narrow smile.

He brushed her fingertips with the cloverleaf and looked into her dark brown eyes.

She looked away and cupped her chin in her hands. "Guess I'm pretty much resigned to the fact that love isn't in the cards for me. I find it very difficult to trust a man anymore. My life's been better without one. That old saying, 'It's better to have loved and lost than never to have loved at all,' doesn't apply to me." Pain lodged in her heart like a shard of glass. A tear formed in her eye and rolled down her face.

Jason traced the tear down her cheek. His rough hand brushed softly against her damp skin as he wiped away the tear.

"I have a good career. I love my home, my dog and my horses. I don't have anyone trying to tell me what to do, or taking my money. I eat and sleep well." She nodded as if trying to convince herself. "I love my life." She took a sip from the bottle and looked out over the still water.

Jason felt her pain. It connected them. "Don't you ever get lonely?"

She leaned back, planting her hands firmly in the plush moss growing in a soft, dense green carpet and stared out across the pond. "Sometimes—not so much anymore—I've learned to accept it."

"It does sound like you've had some rotten luck, but there are good men out there." *One is sitting right next to you, but you just don't realize it.*

"That may be, but I haven't run into them. How 'bout you? Did you find anyone after Francine?"

"Other than Arlene—just a few one night stands. Nothing panned out. I kind of lived like a hermit for a while. Stayed in a friend's cabin out in the woods. Spent a lot of time alone. Really missed my kids. Didn't get to see them very often. I really wasn't very good company back then. Work helped take my mind off the rest of my life."

Carla identified with what he went through and let her guard down. "Would you like to come to dinner Friday night?"

His eyes lit up. "That would be nice. I'd love to come. Thank you for asking."

It was like someone else, not her, had invited him. Her mind raced. *What was I thinking? What am I going to do? Will I be able to do it? I don't know. What will I do with him in my house?* Her stomach churned. She hoped he hadn't detected her unease.

She already regretted opening up to Jason and extending her stupid invitation. She had buried the hurts deep inside of her, not allowed them to surface for years. How had she permitted him to penetrate her carefully established defenses? She was vulnerable, had to protect herself.

Carla sat up straight. Her words were clipped. "I think we should be going. It's a long way back."

"You're right."

He already had a backache, his knee hurt and his butt was killing him. He wasn't looking forward to the ride.

She appeared to be unaffected by aches or pains. She rose quickly, untied her horse and was mounted before he even walked over to Ranger.

Jason realized he wasn't as young or fit as he used to be. Not riding for such a long time certainly contributed to his physical discomfort. He untied Ranger and suppressed a groan as he mounted.

They cantered back, a comfortable gait, easy on the body, and reached their starting point at 4:30. It had been a long day. Carla pulled out a business card and handed it to him. "Call me at work and I'll give you my home address and phone number."

He looked at the card and stuck it in his pocket. "I'll see you next week. Thanks for a great lunch."

"You're welcome. See you." She walked her horse away, Garth panting at their side.

Jason made his way home. It was all he could do to get the horses fed. He trudged stiffly up the steps, stripped off his hat and clothes, turned the faucets on in the shower and let the hot water run. Wet heat soothed his tired, aching muscles. He finished and took two aspirin, then crawled into bed. Carla was the last thing he saw in his mind's eye before he drifted off to sleep.

Carla got home, unsaddled and groomed Angel, and then cleaned the stalls before she fed the horses. She sat in the kitchen sipping a cup of tea when the phone rang.

She looked at the caller ID. "Hi Mom."

"How are things going, dear? I haven't heard from you in a while."

"I know, sorry. I've been busy."

"They still haven't solved the homicides out by you."

"No, they haven't."

"You be careful."

"I am."

"What about that friend you went riding with?" She could hear the smile in her mother's voice. "Have you seen him again? I feel much better knowing you are accompanied by a man in those woods."

"As a matter of fact, he did go with me today. But—he's just a friend. You know how I feel about men."

"Oh, I know what you say, but you're still a very attractive woman and not over the hill by any stretch of the imagination. I bet he's quite interested in you."

"Mommm." Carla paused. "Well then, you should be happy to know I've invited him to dinner."

"Carla, that's wonderful."

"It's just dinner."

"I know there's a nice man for you. Maybe this is the one. Keep an open mind and an open heart."

Carla changed the subject. "I'll stop by and see you next week after work and bring you some fresh vegetables, fruit and berries."

"That will be terrific. I've missed you, and I appreciate anything you bring me out of your garden. When will you be coming? I'll fix dinner."

"How about Tuesday, five-thirty?"

"Perfect. I'll see you then. Bye dear."

"Thanks for calling, Mom." Carla set the handset on the charger.

Her thoughts drifted back to the picnic earlier in the day. His fingers tracing the tear on her cheek. The feel of his hand on hers. *I do feel comfortable around him. Too comfortable.*

# Chapter 8

Renfield and Chandry stood outside the opened door of the interrogation room waiting for the Kitsap County correction's officer to bring in Greg Collier.

A guard brought Collier, wrists cuffed, ankles chained, into the room. His orange prison garb stretched tight across the broad shoulders of his 6'4" 260-pound frame. A black receding hairline showed streaks of gray. Thin lips were barely visible in the mass of grizzled facial hair that hung below the puffy cheeks of his large, round head. Steel gray eyes glared beneath bushy brows. Once the cuffed prisoner was seated at the table, the detectives took the chairs across from him.

"Detective Renfield, my partner, Detective Chandry."

Renfield asked, "What can you tell us about the murders of Tim Sutton and Janice Williams?"

"Never heard of 'em. Don't know anything about murders."

"Yeah, sure." The detective stared straight into the cold eyes.

"That's right." Collier looked directly at Renfield, his expression unchanged.

Renfield didn't take his eyes off the prisoner. "How do you earn a living?"

Collier leaned back in his chair and sneered. "I'm retired."

"Oh, from what? Aren't you a little young to be retired?"

"Nope, I fix cars if I need money." The unblinking eyes stared straight ahead.

Renfield rubbed his chin. "So, you're just a fine, upstanding citizen?"

"That's right."

Chandry stood up, stepped away, then placed his hands on the back of his chair. He leaned over, his eyes even with Collier's. "Maybe you have just a little bit of information that you might share with us to benefit yourself."

"Nope, told you, I don't know any murderers."

Renfield said, "What about all the firearms we found out at your place?"

"We go hunting."

"Yeah, with handguns?" Renfield hit the table with his fist.

"They're for protection."

"From whom?" Renfield leaned across the table.

"Burglars."

Renfield stood up, went to the door and knocked. When the door opened told the guard, "You can take the prisoner back to his cell."

Collier's tone was smug, "You're done with me already?"

Renfield shrugged his shoulders. "No point wasting our time. We've got better things to do."

He watched as Collier was led away. "Come on Rob, we need to get back out to the farm."

Chandry said, "You didn't spend much time on him."

"He wasn't going to tell us anything. Let him stew in a cell for a while. If we find enough evidence, we won't need a confession."

They arrived at Collier's just as a search dog was brought in to look for clues in the murder case. The victims' families had provided items of clothing so the bloodhound could get the scents.

Renfield knew it was a long shot, but he had to try. He owed it to the families of Tim Sutton and Janice Williams. The hound searched around the house and buildings first, but nothing turned up. They moved into surrounding areas, then into the marijuana patch.

On the far side, near the edge of the forest, the dog alerted. Grass was growing through the mesh of a white nylon bag, the kind used for washing lingerie. Dry brown and light colored organic material was in inside.

They photographed and marked the location. Renfield reached with a gloved hand, picked it up, and put it in a plastic bag to bring back to the lab. They followed the dog as the search continued.

Marks on the ground and broken branches continued for a short distance before ending up at a wide spot near the road. Shallow tire tracks indented the dry ground. A car had obviously been parked there some time ago. The dog sniffed, then reacted to a torn plastic Wal-Mart bag that was in a clump of weeds.

Chandry picked up the bag and inspected it. "Looks like dried blood. This must be the execution site."

Renfield tried to wrap his mind around the new findings. The victims were not known to use drugs, but had they stumbled on the field of marijuana and decided to take some home? There were still many more questions than answers.

They marked off this new addition to the crime scene, posted another guard, then finished up and went back to the station with the new evidence.

The detectives began the arduous task of sifting through the evidence. Along with the Pierce County task force, they had bags and bags of mail and personal items to examine. All the material associated with identity theft.

Renfield had a gut feeling they might find something in this mountain of evidence rather than with the meth lab stuff or chop shop. He knew these creeps had something to do with the death of the young couple; he just couldn't make the pieces fit together yet. He was confident it would be solved, but was hoping it would be sooner rather than later, and he wanted to make sure he could make the conviction stick. A gut feeling wasn't enough. He needed hard evidence.

Hours later, it was becoming monotonous. They had to examine each and every envelope and item, and sort them by name. There were hundreds of victims. All the victims had to be contacted. Their credit ratings were at risk, they were open to theft and who knew what else—all because of these scumbags. No matter how long it took, he was determined to put the low lifes away.

Chandry came over and stood next to Renfield, munching on potato chips. "You know, Jim, it's going to take us weeks to go through all this stuff."

"Yeah, taking these guys down will certainly help take a bit of crime out of the area for a while. I just wish it wouldn't leave a vacuum that someone else will fill. I don't think we ever have to worry about running out of work."

"Ain't that the truth? There's no end of bad guys." Chandry held out the bag of chips. "Want some?"

"No thanks."

Chandry returned to his desk and sat down.

Renfield inserted papers into the file cabinet and closed the drawer. "I would love to have my family live in a crime free area, but I can't foresee that happening, not in this lifetime anyway." He picked up another stack of mail, organized it into piles by name in alphabetical order.

"We've been burning the candle at both ends. I'll be relieved when it's over." Chandry stood up and yawned.

"You go home and have a good night. I'll see you in the morning."

Renfield grabbed his blazer and walked out to the parking lot. He climbed into his gold Chevy Malibu, turned the key in the ignition and switched on the radio. His favorite country station was turned on.

Toby Keith was singing "American Ride". Renfield sang along; he knew every word. Finally, he was home after a long day. He turned into his driveway, pressed the button on the remote and drove into the open garage. He barely had a chance to open the door into the house.

"Daddy! Daddy!" Jimmy and Tammy grabbed his legs.

Jimmy said, "Did you get the bad guys?"

He lifted his son in the air and gave him a noisy kiss on the cheek. "I'm working on it."

He set his son down and wrapped his arms around them all. "I missed you."

Paula gave him a hug and kiss. "I'm so glad you're home!"

"Me, too. Thoughts of drugs, thefts, murderers, victims and crime vanished—compartmentalized until the next day.

## Chapter 9

Wednesday afternoon, Jason spent the day checking boundaries and gates. He ran into two girls on horseback and a couple of joggers. Most people were decent, honest folks.

When, he heard rustling a few rows back, he stopped to listen. He moved quietly between the trees and kept his eyes focused on the area to his right. One man was breaking off stems, stripping off the lower leaves and bunching the branches together into "hands" with rubber bands. A stack of green bunched salal was piled nearby. Another man a few rows over worked higher up on the side of the hill.

Jason stepped out and confronted the men. "I need to see your permits."

The first man looked up, but didn't answer. He dropped the stems in his hand. His companion didn't wait for Jason to approach. He took off at a run between the rows, his compadre close behind. Jason stood beside a pile of salal and called the sheriff's department. The next call was to Louis, holder of the brush lease.

"I'll be right out," Louis said.

Immigrant laborers didn't cause any problem as long as they held permits to harvest salal. There was a lucrative market for the evergreen shrub branches that were sent worldwide for their popularity in floral arrangements, a multi-million dollar industry. The plants thrived in the damp, shady forests of the Pacific

Northwest. Several large floral companies located in nearby Belfair, north Mason County and in Kitsap County purchased and processed salal for the booming market.

It was necessary to keep brush from growing between the Christmas trees, so having brush pickers harvest salal was a mutual benefit. Vans dropped off workers at first daylight and parked along the side of the road next to the woods. Laborers banded hands of salal or evergreen huckleberry, hauled armloads of one and a half pound bunches and loaded them into pickups to be transported to buyers. This went on from dawn to late afternoon most of the year throughout west Puget Sound region, except for a couple of months between May and July during "tip" season when the plants put out new growth. Pickers never seemed to run out of the plentiful dark green leaves. They just moved from one area to another.

It was necessary to check their papers. Jason was always on the lookout for illegals without state-issued permits. Abuse of the system was common. He relied on calls from vigilant neighbors to report violations. He knew most of the landowners bordering Northwest Tree Farm land. They had a vested interest in making sure trespassers were kept out. Illegal harvesters habitually used the tree farm as convenient access to their private properties. This was especially true during mushroom season in the autumn.

Chanterelles didn't grow in many places on the tree farms. The bright yellow, deeply gilled mushrooms grew in plentiful patches near salal in deep woods. Pickers harvested them by the bucketful, earning a hefty sum in exchange. Now, late in July he didn't have to contend with that added problem.

Christmas posed a serious threat of tree thieves. November and December he worked a lot of overtime. His patrol of the tree farms was a year-round job.

He used to know all the pickers before immigrants flooded into the area and took over the market. A number of locals knew the backwoods and generations of families had earned their living harvesting native vegetation. Once word got out to the immigrant population, foreigners moved in and quickly took over the industry. Communal housing and shared transportation allowed them to work cheaper, keeping the price of brush down. They held an increasing share of the market, forced out locals who were frustrated when quotas were already met and buyers turned them down. Very few local pickers remained.

The expansive woodlands of Kitsap, Mason and Pierce counties provided a golden opportunity for willing harvesters. Illegals found easy pickings with small chance of being caught. Upon discovery, they abandoned their harvest, vanished into the woods and moved on to a different area.

There were regular lease-holders who had permission to bring crews in. He knew the permit holders, and relied on crew foremen to make sure workers had permits and stayed out of trouble. The tree farms' owners couldn't afford to have trees chopped up along with the salal. Jason checked permits and waved workers on.

Louis drove in and Jason directed him to where the harvested salal lay in bundles. Louis loaded them into the back of his pickup. "I'll be on the look-out for illegals," he promised. "Thanks for letting me know."

Jason waved as the truck drove away. He thought about the crime investigation. He'd heard about the bust on the news and the excavator they'd found. *Just a couple miles down the road from my place. Wonder what they were doing with it. Dave will be glad to get it back.*

He worked toward the section line not far from the main road. "Oh crap."

A new pile of trash was dumped between the trees. He went back to get his truck, drove out and parked as close as he could get. He wrestled a double wide mattress, old model television and an upholstered chair into the truck bed, threw in half a dozen black garbage bags and weighted everything down with seven tires.

Jason slammed the tailgate and leaned against the back, gasped in long deep breaths. Things were getting worse. Too many people couldn't afford to go to the dump. *Sure is a pain in the ass.* He opened a bottle of berry-flavored water and took a break to cool down. Back to normal, he drove back through the gate.

His thoughts returned to Carla. He had been thinking about her ever since they parted company on Saturday afternoon. He took out a notebook, pen, and her business card and punched her number on his cell phone.

After a couple of rings a woman answered the telephone. "Bayview Accounting, Jasmine speaking.

"Can I speak to Carla Summers please?"

"Can I tell her who's calling?"

"Jason Gerard."

"Just a moment please."

He felt his heart beat accelerate, took a few deep breaths and tried to relax.

"Hello, this is Carla Summers."

"Hi Carla, this is Jason."

"Jason—it's good to hear from you. Are you still coming for dinner on Friday?"

"Sure, what time would you like me to be there?"

"How about six-thirty? That will give me time to get things done after work."

"That works for me. I'll bring a bottle of wine."

"That'll be nice." She told him the address and directions.

He knew exactly where she lived. "I'll see you then."

Jason closed his phone and stuck it back in his shirt pocket. He whistled a tune and started back to work.

## Chapter 10

Renfield interlaced fingers behind his head, leaned back in his chair and stared at the ceiling. A struggling fly buzzed, caught in a spider web in the corner. The spider crossed the web toward its victim. Renfield watched the spider with curiosity. *Murder in the homicide department.* He looked away, sat up, and focused his attention on the flat screen monitor on his desktop. The phone interrupted the silence. He answered it after the first ring.

"Jim, Roger Dirndle in the crime lab. We have the test results back from the DNA samples on the cigarette butt and glove you ordered. They're a match."

"Great."

"One more thing. We checked the contents of the mesh bag you brought in. It contained mushrooms."

"Psychedelic mushrooms?"

"No—not hallucinogenic Psilocybin—edible mushrooms: Pleurotus ostreatus, oyster mushrooms and Macrolepiota procera, shaggy parasols. Both species are very tasty."

"Hmm . . . That's interesting. Thanks for getting back to me so soon." He punched the off button.

"Hey, Rob. The DNA results are back. We've got a match!"

"Thank God! That is good news." Chandry's face broke into a grin.

"That's not all. That mesh bag the dog found contained edible mushrooms. The victims must have been pickers. That's got to be the connection. They must have stumbled onto that place by accident and it cost them their lives." Now Renfield had a plausible motive for the murders.

Rob said, "It's about time things started looking up."

"What do you say we take a trip down to the Pierce County jail and interview Freeman again? We can put some real pressure on him now. I think we can get that scumbag to crack. I don't think he's our shooter. I'm not a gambling man, but I bet he's got all the answers that will lead to our perp."

"I'll go along with that. He's a druggie and definitely sleazy, but I don't think he's enough of a hard-ass to do the job. Someone else was the trigger-man. My money's on Collier, but Freeman's definitely involved. I'm sure he helped dispose of the bodies. Let's see what we can wring out of him."

Renfield was hot to get going. "I'll call the Pierce County jail and let them know we're coming."

Traffic was backed up and it was stop and go. It took them an hour and a half to get there. Chandry tapped his fingers on the dashboard as they looked for a place to park. "That Toyota Prius is leaving. Pull in there. Quick! It's a tight squeeze but we'll make it. fit." After a couple of tries they were in.

They locked up and walked briskly to the jail. Soon, an officer brought Michael Freeman into the interrogation room.

"Have a seat." Renfield nodded to the suspect, took the chair opposite, and Chandry took the seat next to his partner.

The prisoner dug his fingernails into the palms of his hands. "Why are you here?"

"We're hoping you'll come clean with us on the Tim Sutton and Janice Williams murders," Renfield started in.

"I told you. I didn't do it. I ain't a killer."

"I'd like to believe you, Mick—I really would. The trouble is now we've got DNA evidence tying you to the crime. We know you were there. You drove the bodies into the pond in an attempt to cover up the murders."

Freeman clenched and unclenched his fists as the color drained from his face.

"I'm innocent, man. I told you, I ain't a murderer."

Renfield's voice was threatening, "You're going to get the death penalty. We're going to make sure you never hurt anyone else."

Beads of sweat broke out on Freeman's forehead and the armpits of his orange prison garb were soaked. "I ain't sayin' nothin'. I want my lawyer."

"Sure. No problem, your attorney's on the way. Would you like a cup of coffee?" Chandry asked.

"Yeah." Freemen rubbed his neck, the irritated skin reddening beneath his hand.

"How 'bout you Jim? Need a cup of java?"

"No thanks. I'm good."

The prisoner swallowed the dark liquid, screwed up his face as the over-brewed coffee coated his tongue.

The door opened and his attorney walked in. "Got here as soon as I could," he said and sat down next to his client.

"About time. Cops are trying to pin a murder on me."

The lawyer placed his briefcase on the table and sat next to his client. "Matthew Creiden, Pierce County Public Defender."

"Detective Jim Renfield, Kitsap County, my partner, Rob Chandry." Renfield fixed his gaze on the lawyer. "The victims were each executed by a single gunshot to the back of the head, hands tied behind their backs. They were put in a car and rolled into a pond. Gloves with your client's fingerprints and DNA and a cigarette butt with his DNA were both found next to the pond where the car went in. We know he's involved in these murders. We're offering to remove the death penalty and reduce the sentence if he comes clean, tells us who the gunman was and agrees to testify in court."

"You don't have a murder weapon. You don't have proof my client murdered anyone."

Renfield said, "We can place him at the scene. That's enough to nail him. If he doesn't talk, anyone else involved may walk. We know more than one person committed this crime. We want all of them, not just this guy."

Freeman looked down at the floor. The half-filled cup of coffee cooled in front of him. His fingers clenched the fabric of his jump-suit while Renfield spoke.

"We know the victims were picking mushrooms near the farm where these guys ran their meth lab and grew marijuana. Those innocent people stumbled on the illegal operation by accident and paid for it with their lives. They were executed to prevent them from disclosing any information about illegal activity."

Renfield looked over at the suspect and stared him in the eye. He raised his voice. "These guys are vicious killers. They pump illegal drugs onto the street. They've stolen the identities of hundreds of people, burglarized homes and businesses, and they run a chop shop for stolen vehicles.

"The families of the murder victims deserve closure. We want to make sure all the perpetrators of this crime are finished terrorizing humanity."

Renfield wanted to make sure Creiden knew exactly what his client was involved in. He didn't leave out anything. He was certain Freeman knew the extent of the illegal activities carried on at Collier's. Even if he wasn't guilty of each and every single crime he certainly had knowledge about the details.

"I need to talk to my client."

"Sure, no problem, we'll be waiting out in the hall." Renfield stretched slowly before getting up. He knocked on the door and the guard opened it. The detective sauntered out leisurely, his eyes on the suspect. He wanted to watch the creep sweat.

Chandry slid his chair back, got up, and stepped out. The door was locked behind them.

Twenty minutes later the attorney called the detectives back.

"No deal. My client is innocent of the murders you're trying to pin on him. He's a drug addict, not a killer. We'll go to trial."

"We can put him at the scene. We don't believe he acted alone. We're offering him his life. Of course, if he would prefer to take his chances, this is a capital offense." Jim looked from the attorney to Michael Freeman.

Freeman swallowed and bit his lip. "I told you, I didn't kill anyone."

"Tell you what. I'll be very generous and give you three days to make a decision. After that, the deal's off the table and we go for the death penalty. You're going to have a new home. We're transferring you to Kitsap County. You and your buddy Greg will be sharing our accommodations."

Freeman's eyes bulged his left eye twitched. He was silent as the guard led him from the room.

"You think three days are going to make any difference?" Chandry asked as they headed to the parking lot.

"I don't know, but I figured it wouldn't hurt to let him stew about it for a while. This guy's a dim bulb. He may need some time to process this. Three days aren't going to make much difference." Renfield pulled out and inched into traffic.

"Yeah, I guess you're right." Chandry swatted a fly beating its wings against the windshield.

"We've still got plenty of evidence to sift through. The ballistics report on the Glock didn't pan out. There's got to be another Glock somewhere." A light turned green, and Jim drove up the on-ramp and merged onto the freeway.

"You know, Rob, they must have dumped the gun. We still haven't found anything belonging to either Janice Williams or Tim Sutton at the farm. All the evidence may have been thrown out."

Renfield thumped his hand on the steering wheel. "There's something we haven't checked. Remember the excavator we found at Collier's place?"

"Yeah."

"What were they doing with it? It wasn't chopped, so they didn't strip it down for parts. They were using that machine for something. Maybe we better take another trip out there and look around. Remember there was a bare patch of ground behind the old barn?"

"You think they buried the evidence?" Rob thought about the area Jim was referring to, and remembered the piece of metal he tried to pull out of the ground.

"It's a possibility. Let's head over there instead of going back to the office."

"Good idea." Chandry pulled a pack of Lifesavers from his pocket and popped one into his mouth. "Want one?" He offered the pack.

"Why not?." Renfield reached for a red candy. "I'm glad Freeman's getting transferred to Kitsap. I hope this is the last time we'll have to make this trip."

Traffic slowed as they crossed the Narrows Bridge and sped up as soon as they reached the other side.

"Yeah, me too. At least we're getting paid to be here. Most of these people commute every day on their own time." Rob looked across at the new bridge. "Traffic's better than it used to be. We should be there in half an hour. I'm glad I don't have to pay the gas and toll often." He crunched up the Lifesaver and took out another. "What do you think about Mrs. Collier? You think she knew this was going on?"

"I don't know. It's hard to imagine how someone could live there and not know. On the other hand, in her condition it's possible." He pulled the turn signal and moved into the next lane as the highway narrowed.

"Yeah, the house was clean. Not a single piece of incriminating evidence in the entire place. Collier wanted to make sure his mother didn't suspect him. Makes you wonder how a nice lady like that could produce such a rotten son."

Rob held up the pack of candy. "Want another?"

"I'm still working on the last one. Collier is some piece of work. I wonder if he ever did an honest day's labor in his life."

They turned into the long driveway and parked near the house next to the duty guard's car. Renfield waved to the guard and showed his badge before proceeding.

They ducked under the crime scene tape. Chandry led the way out back. This time they concentrated on the ground instead of going through vehicles and buildings.

The only disturbed dirt appeared to be an old garden area behind the buildings. Nothing was planted there and weeds were small; the piece of metal still protruded. The detectives scrutinized the excavator's tracks.

"Jim, this looks suspicious, I think we'd better get a heavy equipment operator out here to dig up this site."

Renfield pulled out his cell-phone. "I'll call for one."

Chandry continued to examine the ground while his partner made the call.

Renfield closed the phone. "They'll get one out here as soon as they can. I think we're done for now. Let's take off. We've got to get another warrant. If we hurry, we should be able to get one processed right away. I don't want to have to call a judge in after hours. You know how testy they get about that."

"Yeah."

## Chapter 11

The investigation team waited in the driveway as the truck hauling the excavator showed up, and pulled over alongside. The driver leaned out the window. "Where do you want me to park my rig?"

"You can leave it where it's at," Renfield said.

The driver turned off the motor and jumped down. "I'm, Vince Holt." He started unfastening hooks and chains that tied down the excavator. "Where would you like me to start digging?"

Renfield showed his badge and introduced his partner, then led the way. "Let's walk back. You can decide the best way to proceed." He stopped at the clearing. "This is it."

Vince looked around and studied the track-marred ground. "No problem, I'll drive her up, and we'll get started. Shouldn't take long."

Chandry warned, "You'll have to take it slow and careful. We'll be right here watching. We'll signal you to stop if we spot anything. We don't want to destroy any evidence."

"Gotcha." Vince yanked on the rusty bar sticking out of the ground. "I'll start here, and we'll see what turns up. I'll keep an eye on you. Wave your arms if you see anything." He walked back to the trailer, took his seat in the excavator, and backed down the ramps. The excavator rumbled around the side of the house and came to a stop beside the open space. "Okay, keep back! I don't want to run over anyone."

Chandry stood alongside, but well out of the way. The detectives and two other members of the team with shovels, stood around the edge of the dirt to watch. They didn't have to wait long. It only took a few scoops to expose black plastic.

They waved their arms. The excavator pulled back. The men donned rubber gloves. A member of the team grabbed a garbage bag while another shoveled dirt aside so they could lift it out. It contained ammonia bottles, matchboxes, Sudafed containers, meth lab debris. They set the bag aside and pulled out another with similar contents. After a couple of hours, the team had uncovered half a dozen bags of meth lab waste, but nothing that tied the suspects to the murder investigation.

Chandry finished searching a bag. "I wonder if this dump is going to be full of nothing, but more of this stuff."

Renfield looked out over the rest of the site. "That's certainly possible. Why don't we have the excavator work on the other side? I doubt this stuff was all buried at the same time." He pointed to the far end fifty feet away. "Vince, try over there!"

The excavator scooped up several loads of dirt, revealing pieces of metal, trash and familiar black plastic bags. The team hauled out three more bags. The first two contained more meth materials, but the third looked promising.

One of the guys pulled out a bill-fold, opened it and read the driver's license. "Bingo! We got 'em!"

Everyone stopped.

"What have you got, Brad?" Renfield asked.

"Timothy Sutton's driver's license." Brad handed the license and bill-fold to Renfield.

Renfield examined the items, photographed and bagged them, and then searched through the rest of the garbage bag himself. He lifted out a plain brown purse; scrutinized the contents and removed a beige faux-leather wallet. There was a driver's license with the photo ID of Janice Williams. "Now, we've got connections to both victims."

He opened another bag and took out something wrapped in a grease-covered mechanic's rag. He unfolded the rag and knew he had the murder weapon. "Hey! Look at this!" His hand grasped a 9mm Glock. "What a break! Let's finish digging this up." He bagged all the items.

Renfield logged in the items while Chandry videotaped the entire process. Brad placed yellow markers at the precise locations of the finds.

Chandry was euphoric, better than he'd felt in ages. "We need to get this done while we've got Vince here." The detective pulled more bags over to where the team could go through them. "We're here for the long haul. Okay, Vince, time to get back to work!" Chandry finished going through the last bag disclosing blood-stained clothing and two pairs of shoes. A pair of dirt-covered license plates lay in in the bottom of the bag.

Vince worked for another hour, but no more bags were discovered. The team photographed the scene and items. Renfield diagrammed and logged in meticulous notes. They loaded everything into the investigation van to be hauled to the crime lab. That is, everything except the bags containing bloody clothes, shoes, gun and personal effects associated with the homicide case. The detectives would bring those items in personally, not wanting to risk having them disappear amidst everything else in the evidence room. Renfield wanted to process them immediately. He placed them in the trunk of the car.

Renfield leaned against the excavator. "Great job, Vince, you can take off now."

Vince hollered down. "I need to get you to sign some paperwork first. I'll meet you back at the truck." The excavator turned and disappeared behind the building.

The investigation team was loaded up and ready to go; Renfield and Chandry, last to leave, followed the van out. They arrived at headquarters, and carried the bags to the crime lab. Samples were taken for analysis.

The day still wasn't over. They began the arduous task of tackling the inevitable paperwork that accompanied everything they did. Jim hated paperwork, but this time, he attacked that dreaded chore with more enthusiasm than normal.

## Chapter 12

Carla left work early. She was stressing out over dinner that night. It wasn't the actual meal she was worried about. An excellent cook, she had everything she needed to prepare a sumptuous meal. It was the thought of having a man in her house again that unnerved her.

Every man she ended up with turned out to be worse than the last. Physically or mentally, she couldn't afford another bad relationship. After she finally got rid of Walter, she swore she would never let another man into her life.

She had a good career. It got busier than she liked at tax time, but most of the time it wasn't too bad. She could schedule time off if she needed to. She lived in a nice home on her farm with her horses and dog. A man would only screw up her life.

She had let her guard down somehow. She wasn't even sure how it happened. She just knew she'd been careless, and was going to have to get through the evening without getting in any deeper.

Jason did seem nice, so far, anyway. That was the problem. Men always started out nice. It was only after you let one into your life, fell in love and committed yourself, that the metamorphosis occurred. She had plenty of experience with that. They started out treating her like a queen and ended up treating her like a doormat. She led a contented life. Animals never asked for much. They were devoted, appreciative, and always happy to see her. They caused her no grief unless one got sick or died. She loved working with them. Life without them was unimaginable, so contrary to life with a man.

She was at peace with her decision to remain on her own, but now here she was, breaking her promise to herself. *I'm weak. I gave in.*

A small part of her still believed in the fairytales of her youth: fall in love and live happily ever after. In spite of her history, no matter how hard she tried, she was unable to completely eradicate the desire buried deep within her psyche for a relationship. It remained buried, a small seed, still able to sprout. It never really died.

She feared she was heading down that road again. *What an idiot! Why don't I ever learn? I'll survive tonight, and make sure things don't go any farther.* She just needed to summon up the courage and willpower to hold out. She knew she was not good at that. It would take every bit of her inner strength and resolve, but it was necessary for her salvation. If she felt herself slipping, she would think of Walter. That should do the trick. Now that she had a plan, she felt better.

Garth sensed something was wrong. He whined, walked over and licked her hand.

She wrapped her arms around the big dog and hugged him close. "You're always here for me aren't you, boy?" She let him go and started to change her clothes.

Comfortable blue jeans replaced a gray, calf-length skirt. Her feet felt free at last in a pair of tennis shoes, no longer imprisoned in the pantyhose and moderately high-heeled gray shoes. A loose-fitting gray tee-shirt with the slogan, "*Uppity Women Unite*" emblazoned across the front in large red letters replaced the jacket and flowered blouse. She ran a brush through her hair, then headed to the barn.

The horses saw her coming, and whinnied greetings. Food was always at the forefront of their concentration and today wasn't any different. The black colt, Shazan, frolicked in the corral, kicking up his heels and running near his mother. His coat contrasted with dapple-gray Geisha. Angel looked toward Carla with those deep brown eyes. A layer of dust lightened the dark brown of her coat. Carla walked into the barn and the horses entered their stalls grumbling. She scooped grain into the feeders and tossed hay into the racks.

The calming effect of being with the horses started to wear off as Carla walked back to the house. She went in just long enough to wash her hands and get a basket before she went to the garden.

Her nerves calmed slightly as she cut broccoli, chard and spinach, broke off lettuce leaves—green leaf, red leaf, and romaine, arugula. Lots of green tomatoes hung on the vines. They wouldn't be ready for a few more weeks, sometime in August.

The chickens clucked from inside their pen, ran back and forth along the wire. She looked at them.

"All right." She broke off a few more lettuce leaves and tossed them in to the hens.

Carla laughed as the birds tumbled over each other in their rush to get to the fresh food. They surrounded the lettuce, tore off shreds and ate greedily. She left the chickens, stopped at the raised bed of herbs near the house and broke off some rosemary, tarragon and fresh thyme before going inside.

Carla laid the vegetables and herbs on the table, seasoned the pork roast and inserted it on the rotisserie. She prepared the rest of their meal while the meat roasted. A loaf of bread was almost done in the bread machine. She had put the ingredients in before she went to work and set the timer. Taking out more containers, she headed back outside to pick berries. Blueberries, raspberries and strawberries were all ripe for the tart she planned to make. The ever-bearing varieties would produce all summer.

It was nearly 6:30 and she was almost done. Her concerns, temporarily subsided while she was busy in the kitchen, began to creep back into her consciousness. She was running out of time. Jason would be here soon. Her anxiety increased with each passing minute.

Garth started barking before she heard the sound of the vehicle in the driveway; nose to the door, his barking intensified with the sound of footsteps. The doorbell rang.

"Garth, quiet." Carla held onto his collar as she opened the door.

The dog's behavior changed instantly. His tail wagged in eager greeting and he pressed his nose against Jason's leg. Jason rubbed the dog's head behind his ears and Garth moaned in pleasure.

"Garth, go lie down," Carla commanded.

The shepherd reluctantly went to his corner and curled up on his bed.

"He's just happy to see me."

"I know, but he isn't supposed to bother people." Her voice sounded sharper than she intended.

"He wasn't bothering me. I don't mind. I love dogs."

"Well, I expect him to behave." It irritated her that Garth was so eager to accept this man as a friend. He was her devoted companion and he wasn't normally so willing to befriend another person.

Jason followed Carla into the kitchen. Garth watched him from his bed in a corner. The aroma of roasted meat and fresh-baked bread filled the room.

Jason handed Carla a bottle of wine. "It smells wonderful in here."

"Thank you. Dinner is nearly ready to serve." The table was set and all she had to do was carve the meat. "Go ahead and have a seat."

"Sure, as soon as I uncork the wine."

She handed him a corkscrew and watched how expertly he used it, like a waiter in a fine restaurant.

He removed the familiar cap and sat down at the table. For the first time, she saw wavy brown hair silvering around the temples.

She brought platters of food and poured wine into crystal glasses before sitting across from him. "Help yourself. Let's eat while it's hot."

He raised his glass and they clinked a silent toast. Then he filled his plate. "I'm a pretty good cook, but I'm usually so tired after work, I don't bother. I seldom get the chance to enjoy a real meal. I know I should eat healthier, it's just not often convenient." He took a forkful of meat and chewed slowly. "Mmmm, this practically melts in your mouth."

"Thank you, I raised it myself. I buy a couple of wiener pigs every year. The butcher shop in town does a great job. They make excellent sausage and hams. Good nutrition is important for good health. I don't trust processed foods. I know what I eat is organic, safe, and healthy." She took a sip of wine, and then buttered a slice of bread.

Jason looked out the window and saw the horses in the corral. "Everything here is so organized and so well kept, like a picture-perfect postcard."

"I work in my yard and garden almost every day. Weeds get out of control if I don't. It's much easier to keep up with things if I stay on top of it." She lifted a forkful of broccoli to her mouth. "What do you do in your spare time?"

He sipped his wine and set down the glass. "Spare time? I don't have much of that. I'm always working."

"How about your family? When do you see them?"

Jason ate the last bite of meat on his plate and helped himself to more pork and another slice of bread. "My son Jeff and his wife Cindy have two kids. Anthony is four and Marie is three. They are always busy. With my schedule I don't see them very often. Becky teaches fifth grade. Her husband Ken is an engineer at Boeing. They have a son, Jason, my namesake, who just turned two. I wish we had more time together. Every time I see my grandkids they've changed so much."

He tilted the empty wine glass, set it down and refilled it. He held out the bottle. "Would you like some more?"

"No thank you. I'm fine." *I certainly don't want to drink too much.* "What about your parents?"

He leaned back in his chair and took a sip of wine before he spoke. "Mom and Dad live in Seattle in the same house I grew up in. They're still able to get around and take care of themselves, but I worry about them." He looked down at his plate where his second helping of food remained untouched. He picked up his knife and fork and cut up a piece of meat. "I guess I've been talking too much. How about you? Do you have family here?"

Carla held her empty fork poised in mid-air. "My father grew up in Kansas, joined the Navy and ended up being stationed in Bremerton. He liked it here, so decided to stay and worked at the shipyard until he retired. My mother grew up in Port Orchard in a house not far from the beach. After my grandparents died, we moved into their house. I've never lived anywhere else. I love West Puget Sound. Dad had a stroke a few years ago and passed away a year later. Mom still lives alone in the same house. I try to see her every couple of weeks, but I've been so busy lately, I haven't spent as much time with her as I'd like to. I speak to her on the phone several times a week." She remembered the last call and her mother's words. *"Keep an open heart."* She pushed the last bite of meat around her plate.

They finished their meal and sipped wine until the bottle was empty. Carla wasn't used to drinking often and felt a little lightheaded. She got up to clear the table. He started to help. She took the stack of plates from him. "Are you ready for dessert?"

"I can't eat another bite right now. How about we take a walk outside and you show me your place?"

"Sure." She was proud of her farm, especially her latest edition, Shazan. Getting Jason out of the house and into the yard and barn seemed safer somehow. Garth slipped out the door ahead of them.

She led Jason past the garden and chicken house to the two story classic red horse barn, complete with white trimmed double Dutch doors. The horses trotted up as they noticed people walking toward them.

Jason let out a whistle as he watched the long-legged black colt cavorting between the older pair. He had the fine lines of a real showstopper. His dam was a very classy dapple-gray. Her nostrils flared, taking in Jason's scent; her ears flicked forward, listening to his soft-spoken words. The fine-boned head, so characteristic of the breed, turned to nuzzle the colt that moved up and pressed against her far side.

Shazan stood back, unsure of the stranger at the fence. He bolted off with a snort, kicking up his heels and running in circles before returning to his mother's side.

They both laughed at the colt's antics. Carla could always count on Shazan to be entertaining. She could watch him for hours. He was her pride and joy. She loved to lead him around, and to run her hands over the firm muscles, getting him used to human touch. He allowed her to lift his feet, cleaning out the tiny hooves. Her farrier would appreciate the effort she spent on this training when it came time for him to be shod. She looked forward to training him as he grew.

Jason looked the horses over carefully. "They're awesome," he said with true admiration. "You have a lot of money and time invested in them." Many men would have resented the time, not to mention the expense. Jason sounded impressed.

"They are my passion. I've put my heart and soul into them." Carla turned to leave the barn. "Are you ready for dessert yet?"

"Sure." He followed her. "Would you mind if I just take a look around outside for a few minutes?"

"No. Go right ahead—take your time. Come back in whenever you're ready."

He turned away without seeing the relief on her face. She would have some time alone without having to worry about what to do or say. It wasn't that he was difficult to talk to. Actually, conversation with him was easy. That's what worried her. She didn't want to let her guard down. So far, she was in control of the situation and wanted to make sure she kept it that way.

Back inside, Carla rinsed the dishes and loaded the dishwasher. She was slicing the tart when she heard the sound of footsteps on the porch. Garth, the traitor, had stayed out with Jason, preferring to shadow him rather than come in with her. Oh, well, Garth did like to be outside. He bounded in ahead of Jason, who took his seat at the table.

"That looks scrumptious." He spooned some whipped cream over his tart and tasted the first bite. "Mmmm. That is delicious. Are those berries all out of your garden?"

"Yes. Since so much food is imported from foreign countries now, it's more incentive to grow my own. I usually raise a couple of steers and sell the extra meat. You must have noticed my laying hens. I also buy Cornish Cross chicks to raise for fryers.

I have a friend who grows all his own food, too. Sometimes I buy from or barter with him. It's sad to see the decline of family farms. I'm doing my best to remain self-sufficient and continue to raise public awareness for the need for local farms." She stopped talking and popped a whipped cream covered strawberry into her mouth.

"That's impressive, especially since you live alone. I noticed the trees in the orchard. They look in pretty good shape. A few branches could use some pruning."

"I do all the pruning myself."

"How can you keep up with everything? That's a lot of work for one person."

"I'm not superwoman." She laughed. "I hire a boy to help out with the heavier chores. I'm lucky I have a great career that enables me to live as I choose."

"I don't have to rely on support from another person. I'm quite capable of supporting myself."

"Do you ever wish you had a partner to enjoy all this with?" He regretted the words as soon as he spoke.

Carla stared down at her plate, a mouthful of berries swirling around on her tongue. *Oh, no, now what?* She couldn't talk with her mouth full. She delayed swallowing to give herself time to think.

At last she spoke in a flat voice. "Been there, done that." She took another bite.

He got the impression she didn't want to discuss it further, so he let the topic drop. They finished eating the last of dessert in silence.

He stood up from the table and laid his hand on hers. "I have to get up very early to meet my boss in the morning. Would you be offended if I take off so soon after dinner?" He didn't have to leave yet, but he sensed his remark had made her uncomfortable, so he decided to give her some space and leave earlier than planned.

"Not at all." She didn't intend to sound quite so relieved.

"How about if I call you?"

She hesitated before answering. "That would be fine." She walked outside with him.

He touched her shoulder and gave her a quick kiss on the cheek. "Thank you for a really great dinner. I had a terrific time." Without another word, he got into his truck and drove slowly down the driveway.

She watched him go and her fingers brushed her flaming cheek where he'd kissed her. Suddenly, her mind was muddled. The tiny part of her that craved companionship caused conflict inside her head. She returned to the house and cleaned the kitchen, then sat on the sofa and flipped through the channels on TV.

She had come to accept her life alone and this man had started to chip away, if only a fraction, at the thick wall she'd built up to preserve her well-being. It was unsettling. She didn't want to admit that part of her hoped that maybe, just maybe, he wasn't like all the other men she'd let into her life.

Nothing on TV looked interesting so she decided to go to bed. For hours, she tossed and turned, rearranged her pillow, and felt his lips on her cheek. Tormented sleep came hours later. She woke up exhausted the next morning.

## Chapter 13

Jim Renfield rifled through the latest crime lab reports. Both sets of tennis shoes were a match for the footprints found next to the pond. DNA test results on those and the clothes weren't finished yet.

A phone rang down the hall. The sheriff's voice penetrated the thin walls. "Hey, we're working our tails off down here. My detectives are on top of this thing. It takes time. When I have something to report, you'll be the first to know." He slammed the phone down. "Damn!"

The door opened and Sherriff Wheeler walked over and leaned on Renfield's desk. "How's the investigation coming, Jim? Getting any closer to wrapping the thing up?"

"Ballistics reports on the gun found at the dig verified it was the murder weapon. Unfortunately, it was wiped clean of prints. The registered owner reported it stolen in a residential burglary more than two years ago. That cold case will be solved soon."

"Hmmm. Well, that's a benefit. But, reporters are on my ass. The press want this case solved, yesterday."

"I know." Renfield closed his eyes, laced his fingers behind his neck and stretched his back and neck muscles. "Finally, we've had some lucky breaks: the discovery of the bodies by the tree farm patrolman, and the amazing stupidity of the convenience store burglar. That someone would actually steal lottery tickets, then try to collect on them is beyond comprehension." He made no attempt to conceal a grin. "But the fact that the idiot was tied to the homicides as well as a multitude of other crimes is providential. God must have had a hand in helping us."

Wheeler thumped his hand on the brown laminate desktop. "Well, we'll take all the help we can get to wrap this up in a nice tidy package. I'm up for reelection next year. Getting this case put to rest ASAP without a bunch of cost overruns would certainly help."

Renfield unlaced his fingers and sat forward. "We're doing our best."

"I know you are. See if you can build a fire under those guys in the lab. Get those DNA results back."

Renfield leaned forward, reached for the phone, tried to suppress the sarcasm in his voice. "I'll work on that."

Wheeler turned away and returned to his office. "Keep me in the loop." The door shut behind him.

Renfield opened the top door of his desk, pulled out a pack of Rolaids, popped two into his mouth.

Chandry got out of his chair, sauntered over to Chandler's desk and eyed the pile of photos on Renfield's desk. "Pressure's on."

"Yeah, like we didn't have enough already."

Rob ate a bite of a sandwich and nodded toward the hall. "Cut him some slack. He's under the gun. We do the work, but his ass in on the line. Don't take it personal."

"I know. Been doing this a long time." Jim looked at his partner and touched his index finger to his own chin. "You've got a blob of mustard on you."

Rob pulled a napkin out of the lunch sack and dabbed his face. "Did I get it?"

"Nope, other side."

Rob wiped again, looked at the yellow streak on the napkin. "How's that? Did I get it?"

"Yep, you're good." Jim pulled his chair closer to the desk. "It's time to go see our perp, Freeman, over at the Kitsap jail, wouldn't you say?"

"Yep, it all seems to be coming together with or without him, but it sure would speed things up if he'd cooperate."

"It could tie up some loose ends. I think we ought to give it a try. We have enough facts to entice Freeman to confess. Now that we've moved him up here to Kitsap County let's hope his new lawyer can convince him to come clean." Jim picked up the phone, ran through the numbers. "I'll call Dale Tyson so we can set up an appointment. No point wasting time waiting for him to show up."

A few hours later they walked into the interrogation room. Attorney Tyson and his client were already seated, waiting for them. They slid up chairs and sat across the table.

"Mr. Freeman, how are you today?" Renfield pulled a recorder out of his pocket and turned it on. He set it down and locked eyes with Freeman.

"I'm okay." Freeman grimaced, fidgeting in his chair.

Renfield spoke slowly, didn't take his eyes off the prisoner. "We've uncovered all the evidence you guys buried out at Collier's farm. It would be in your best interest to come clean."

Tyson spoke first. "My client maintains his innocence."

Renfield paused, glanced briefly at Tyson, then glared unblinking at Freeman. "The victims were executed by gunshots to the back of the head, deep-sixed into a pond. Do you think a jury's going to be sympathetic? If you're willing to testify against Collier, we'll talk to the prosecutor about reducing the charges. That's your best chance."

Freeman bit his lip and looked away.

Tyson said, "Let me talk to my client."

Renfield said, "Sure, you can have twenty minutes."

Renfield shoved his chair back and stood up. He headed out to the coffee stand. Chandry was right behind him. They each got a latte and sat on a wooden bench.

Chandry stirred his cup and took a sip. "Let's hope this dirtbag does the right thing for once in his life. Maybe he's getting desperate. He's running out of options. This was a horrific crime. These guys are a plague on society. I don't think there's a jury anywhere that would let these guys off. We've got a mountain of evidence against them."

Renfield leaned back rested his head against the wall. "There's no way they can afford a dream team for defense. They have a public defender. Besides, these weren't your average run-of-the-mill bad guys. They executed an innocent couple; they're dead meat."

He remembered playing little league baseball. He could almost hear the crowd cheering in the stands as he rounded third base, then slid home, breaking the tie and winning the game. He'd been on top of the world then. This was beginning to feel almost as good.

"But we need a confession to nail Collier." Chandry drained his cup and tossed it into a wastebasket.

"I agree. Freeman can name him as the shooter. That's the piece of the puzzle we're missing. It's got to come from this jerk. There's no way we'll ever get Collier to crack. That guy's tough as nails." Renfield looked at his watch, and crumpled his cup before sending it into the bin on top of his partner's. "Come on, time's almost up."

The guard unlocked the door and the detectives took their places across from Freeman and the PD.

"Well, are you willing to cooperate in order to avoid the death penalty or shall we continue with this in court?"

"My client is innocent. He never murdered anyone. He wants to take his chances with a jury trial." Tyson's voice sounded skeptical. It was obvious he didn't agree.

Renfield bolted out of his chair. "Okay, if that's the way you want it, we'll see you in court." He knocked and the door opened.

Chandry was up and the pair strode out the door, closed it behind them.

The P.D. stared at his client who had expected the detectives to try to persuade him to co-operate. Unless they were bluffing, their swift departure was an indication they were feeling confident of a conviction. His client was an idiot for not taking the offer.

As they walked back to their office, Renfield spoke for both of them. I bet we could have wrung a confession out of that scumbag if we'd had him alone. It's all coming down so slick."

Chandry said, "Maybe it's not so simple. Why is Freeman protecting Collier? Out of loyalty? I doubt it. I think he's afraid of his old friend, probably for good reason. I'm sure we're going to be able to nail these guys. We have so much evidence. We just have to make sure we do our homework. Dot every i and cross every t. I don't want these creeps to get off because we screwed up somewhere." Chandry took a pack of lifesavers out of his pocket and popped a yellow one into his mouth. He held out the pack. Want one?"

"Yeah, sure." Renfield took the roll and removed a green one. "Thanks." He handed the pack back. "I think we better go through all those files again. I want this case to be ironclad that Collier's the shooter."

"My gut is telling me the same thing. We still have a whole lot of legwork to do to get this case tied up. The evidence is there. We just have to get it all sorted and make sure we don't leave out anything. What about the other people we rounded up? You think any of them know anything?"

"No, doubtless they were involved in a lot of criminal activity, but we haven't found one thing to connect anyone else to the homicides."

Renfield stood beside his desk and looked at the picture of Paula and the kids. "Rob, I don't know about you, but I say let's make it a short day and get a fresh start in the morning. It's been a long time since we put in a normal shift."

"Sound's good to me. With all the extra time we've been putting in, it will be nice to get home early."

"I'm going to give Paula a call and let her know I'll be home for dinner. That'll be a nice surprise. We'll hit the ground running tomorrow."

## Chapter 14

Jason walked down a road between the trees. He looked up at the gunmetal gray sky; the color matched his mood. Drizzly days melted into one another, forming a monotonous gray blur of passing time. July was normally dry, but this was one of those damp summers so overpublicized about the Pacific Northwest.

He'd been working ten hours a day, seven days a week. Lots of people were riding, walking, or running through the farm land. He had to make sure everyone had permits and they weren't doing anything to cause trouble.

It took more than eight years of hard work and careful cultivation to grow quality trees that commanded premium prices. Tree maintenance workers pruned and sprayed, tractors with mowers maintained vegetation between the rows, and brush pickers continuously worked their way from one area to another between rows of noble, grand, or sheared Douglas fir, all destined for their one short purpose in life.

Many would be cut, baled and loaded into containers to be sent overseas to help provide a joyous Christmas for the many thousands of American military families stationed around the world. Japan, South Korea, Philippines, Guam and Hawaii all received trees from Pacific Northwest tree farms. A large volume of trees made their way into Washington's homes.

This booming agricultural industry thrived in West Puget Sound.

The whole year's work came down to profits from Christmas sales. Good years or bad, the business had to subsist on that income until the next year. Jason was the one person out there making sure the trees and land were secure.

A voice broke the silence. He stopped, listened—heard another voice, deeper. Jason crouched, moved silently between the trees. The sounds were closer, but came from way off the path. Something caught his attention.

"What the . . . ?" He emerged from behind the trees into a small clearing.

Two small children, a man and woman sat on folding chairs in front of a green dome tent.

Jason was flabbergasted. His voice sounded harsher than he meant. "What are you doing here? This isn't a campground!"

The woman gasped. Her hand flew to her mouth. She reached for a little girl and pulled the child against her.

The man's chest heaved as he sighed deeply. His stained plaid flannel shirt opened where a button was missing at the chest. His voice was low, soft; the words came slowly. "I know . . . We're not hurting anything . . . got nowhere to go." He took a deep breath. "Name's Mike." He nodded toward the woman. "My wife Claire. I'm a carpenter, been out of work for over a year . . . Don't get unemployment . . . Lost our home."

Jason looked at the woman. Tears flowed down her hollow cheeks leaving damp streaks through grime. He struggled with words. "I'm sorry. You can't stay here."

A small boy wearing a red hoodie with Mickey Mouse on the front pointed at him. "Who's that?"

"Jason Gerard, tree patrolman for Northwest Tree Farm." He noticed the boy's small filthy fingers, thought of his grandson. *He must be about the same age as Anthony.*

The woman wiped her cheek with the sleeve of her turquoise windbreaker. "What'll happen to us?"

"I've got to call the Sherriff and tell them you're here. Sorry."

Jason stuffed his hands in his pockets, jingled some coins. He pulled out his phone, speed dialed and explained the situation.

"Someone will be here soon."

Mike lifted the tent flap and ducked inside. He handed out two full black garbage bags. "Claire, take these outside."

His wife set them beside a tree. A few minutes later four rolled up sleeping bags, a box of food, a doll and a toy truck were added to the pile. Mike pulled out the tent stakes and took apart the frame. Jason helped him fold it up.

The phone rang. "Jason Gerard." He listened for a minute. "I'll be there in a few minutes to let you in." He looked at Mike. "I've got to go let the deputy in. I'll be right back." He jogged to his truck and bumped down the rutted road.

Deputy Stevens was sitting in the county Sherriff's car parked at the gate. Jason jumped out of the truck and unlocked the cable and walked over to the side of the vehicle.

"Hi Tom."

"What have you got Jason?"

"Family of four homeless people. That's a first."

"Sign of the times. Been seeing a lot of homeless people lately. Pretty sad. Especially the ones with kids."

"Yeah." Jason wiped his eyes. "What's the word on the murder investigation?"

"You heard they arrested a couple of guys, Michael Freeman and Greg Collier."

"Yeah, they just lived a couple of miles down the road from me. I know the Collier family. Nora's a nice lady. She used to be a cashier at the grocery in Key Center. That was before they put her on oxygen. Her husband Frank died a three or four years ago."

I never had much to use for Greg. He's an ass. Saw Freeman a couple of times at Spuds and Suds. A real loser. Wasn't hard to avoid them. I don't get into town much."

"We'd better get back there."

"I'll follow you."

Mike and Claire sat side by side, the little boy, on hands and knees pushed a Tonka truck across the ground. The little girl clutched her doll and leaned against her mother.

Jason stood back while Deputy Stevens talked to the family. Half an hour later, Steven's motioned to Jason. "They've got a van parked out near the road. Think you can haul their possessions out? I'll drive the family. Think I can get them into a homeless shelter for a couple of nights. They'll have to work things out after that."

"Sure, no problem." Jason helped Mike lift everything into the bed of his pickup.

Stevens opened the back doors of the car and the family got in.

Jason said, "I'll follow you, but I need to stop and lock the gate."

They pulled up behind a Silver Chevy Astro nearly hidden in the woods. Jason helped unload their gear. "I've got to get back to work." He shook Mike's hand, and then took out his wallet and removed a bill, handed it and some spare change to Mike. "Here's twenty bucks. "Good luck."

"Yeah, hey, thanks."

"You're welcome."

Jason waved. "See you, Tom."

Deputy Stevens touched the brim of his hat and got into the patrol car.

Jason returned to the abandoned campsite. He scrutinized the ground. A plastic grocery bag with a couple of empty water bottles was caught in the lower limbs of a sheared fir. He untangled it and started back to his truck. A glimpse of something yellow caught his attention. He reached down, picked up a matchbox car and spun the tiny wheels. *Little boy's going to miss this.* He stuffed it into his Gortex jacket pocket.

He set the bag in the truck cab and went back to work examining trees. His thoughts drifted away from the family and tree farm, back to a slender, buxom figure astride an elegant bay Arabian prancing at a high-stepping trot, tail carried high and flowing. He could see them in his mind's eye; how glorious they were, gliding between the trees as one.

He knew Carla was wounded. Not in the physical sense, but her emotional pain was very real. He could see it in her eyes. It wasn't so much in the words she spoke, but more in what she left unsaid.

He didn't want to rush into a relationship either. She wasn't the only one suffering from invisible scars. He felt vulnerable, carrying his own share of emotional baggage. Funny, how age helped put it all into perspective.

He thought of youth so full of innocence and optimism. Divorce, death, financial struggles: none of those figure into our expectations as we start out on our independent lives to face unforeseen pitfalls, unimaginable to the invincible eyes of the young.

The illusion of the fairytale still exists: get married, raise a family, grow wealthy with age, and retire to a life of leisure. Sometimes, the live-happily-ever-after part disintegrates along the way.

There were lots of couples out there who did make it. He'd see them together and wondered how they had managed to have lasting, loving relationships.

He had expected to be in that category, never imagined he'd be different. But here he was, alone. He was grateful to have two great kids and, so far, three grandkids. They were the best things to come from his life, but something was missing. He longed for more.

He lived almost as a hermit after Francine left, stayed in a cabin on Hood Canal and worked for the tree farm. For a couple of years he barely existed, avoided human contact as much as possible, ran from life the only way he knew how. It was survival and it got him through.

*I'm stronger now. It's amazing how pain strengthens the soul.* He even lost weight, but would never recommend divorce as a diet plan.

Random thoughts pushed aside, he summoned up courage, reached for the cell phone in his pocket and speed-dialed her number. His stomach rolled as the secretary answered. He asked to speak to Carla.

"Hello, Carla Summers."

His heart raced. "Hi Carla. It's Jason. Are you busy?"

"I can talk for a few minutes."

"I was just wondering if you would like to go riding with me next Saturday." He took a deep breath as he waited for her reply.

"Sure, that would be fun."

"Shall we meet at eight-thirty? We're usually there by then anyway." He was breathing easier.

"I'll bring lunch again."

"See you then."

"Bye."

Jason walked among the trees and whistled a nameless tune. Butterflies in his stomach settled down. A light drizzle fell and moistened his skin, but didn't dampen his spirits.

Carla pushed her chair away from her desk, and leaned back. *What's wrong with me? I did it again. Why don't I stop and think before I open my mouth? I can't believe I agreed to see him again so soon. Why can't I just say no?*

She got up, walked over to the window and watched bumble bees gather nectar from the profusion of red and white rose blossoms. Beads of water collected on the petals, glimmering jewels on this dull day.

Her mind drifted. How confident and in control she felt riding, her horse responding to her commands. *Why can't I have as much control over my own emotions? I've already lost sleep over him. No way I'm letting him get closer. He's just a friend.* She needed to make sure it stayed that way. It wasn't that she had any problem with him.

That was the trouble. He was too nice. She pushed thoughts of him aside and went back to work.

## Chapter 15

They plodded along at a leisurely pace for a couple of hours and passed the pond without stopping. Since the murders, the peaceful setting had lost its appeal, memories of the dead still intruded into the present. They continued riding up to the top of the plateau.

A bald eagle circled overhead; the great bird glided several times around before it disappeared beyond the trees. Swallows twittered and swooped, pursuing fleeing insects. A chipmunk stuffed seeds into its cheek pouches as it perched on a small stump, a fir cone clutched in its paws. It dropped its prize and ran up a tree scolding as Garth bounded up.

They rode several more miles Jason pulled up on the reins and Ranger stopped. "Shall we head back? We can stop for lunch on the way."

"Sure, that's fine with me." She wheeled Angel and rode beside Jason at a slower pace than they'd ridden out.

He turned down a side road half an hour later. "I'm ready for a break.

"Good idea."

They dismounted and tied the horses to a tree. Carla handed Jason a bottle of water and sandwich, placed a plastic bowl of cookies between them, then joined him on the familiar log.

They ate in silence for a while and finished their sandwiches and listened to bird calls and the repetitious drumming of a nearby woodpecker. All the problems in the world seemed to dissipate as they sat there in the intoxicating air.

Jason looked into the distance. She bit into a cookie and chewed slowly.

He brushed crumbs off his pant leg. "How did you end up breeding Arabians?"

"I've loved horses my whole life, ever since I first rode a pony at the Puyallup Fair when I was five. I could never have one of my own until I finished college, and could afford my own place in the country. My first horse, Cheyenne, was an Appaloosa. She was well-mannered, but I had friends who had Arabs and I loved the shape of their heads, conformation, and spirited personalities.

"I bought my first one more than ten years ago. I've had Geisha for a couple of years. She's the best brood mare I could find." She sipped a drink of water.

"Shazan is my first foal." Her eyes sparkled in the sunlight, a grin on her lips. "It has been very exciting from the day he was born. I work with him every day. Horses are the most beautiful animals. I get so much pleasure from them."

Dimples accentuated her cheeks as she spoke with animation about her equine loves. Jason noticed her mood was relaxed and cheerful whenever she talked about her horses.

Garth took a break from sniffing the ground and pressed his head against Jason's leg. Jason leaned down to rub the base of the dog's soft ears. The dog shifted his muzzle and held his chin up for a rub. Jason moved his hands beneath the raised head.

"I know what you mean. I feel the same way. It's hard to put into words. There is something special about horses. I got them for my kids, but I ended up loving them as much as Becky and Jeff did. I haven't ridden much the past few years, but I still like having them around. I enjoy riding with you."

Carla tossed a piece of cookie near the stump. The chipmunk worked its way down from the safety of the tall tree, moving cautiously in halting jerky spurts as it paused to check for danger before approaching the unexpected offering. It sniffed the cookie, then sat up to eat, holding the food in its paws as it took small bites, eyes alert in case Garth noticed and made an effort to pursue. Unmolested, the striped rodent consumed its meal and retreated back up the tree.

Carla listened to Garth moan with pleasure, noticing how content he looked as he submitted to Jason's ministrations. A twinge of irritation gnawed at her as she forced the emotion aside. "How about your ex-wife, does she like to ride?"

"Yeah, we often rode together. She used to spend a lot of time taking the kids to 4-H. It was a good time for all of us. That's what makes it so hard to understand why she left. I guess I was working too much. I didn't notice things were going haywire until it was too late." He looked down at the ground, his eyes watering. "It was a hard lesson."

Carla's own suppressed feelings emerged. "I still feel a lot of guilt about Randy's drug use. I felt responsible; like it was my fault. I went through a lot of counseling. I finally realized it wasn't anything to do with me and cut myself loose. I don't know what happened to him—if he's even alive. It was very hard to recover. In some ways, I never have." Her eyes shifted to the ground and focused on a trail of ants that moved small crumbs, bits of their lunch that were not going to waste.

"I dated a number of men after that, but I could never find anyone to take Randy's place. He was the love of my life. I just hated dating so much; I gave up looking and stupidly married the first man who seemed tolerable—Walter." Even after all this time his name seemed to catch in her throat and conjure up negative images as the man resurfaced, violating the tranquility of the setting. "It was the dumbest decision I ever made in my life." She shuddered and closed her eyes.

Jason noticed the change in her demeanor. He reached over and laid his hand on her shoulder. She opened her eyes and looked away. He removed his hand.

She continued. "He was nice enough at first, but there wasn't the chemistry I had with Randy. We got along for a while, then things went downhill. He didn't like riding and seldom went with me. He was very jealous, and didn't trust me at all. He was even jealous of the horses and the time I spent with them. I never met anyone as selfish and self-centered as he was. He carried so much anger, and became difficult and controlling. When verbal abuse turned physical, I got a restraining order and ordered him out."

Her expression brightened. She whispered, "Look," and pointed to where a doe emerged from between the trees a hundred feet away.

The deer eyed them. She stopped and watched, ears turning, listening. A pair of white-spotted fawns moved out to join their mother and followed her closely as the trio bounded off and vanished behind a row of trees.

They watched the deer in silence before Carla continued," I just can't stand the thought of going through that again." A tear ran down her cheek, and she wiped her eye with her hand.

"My dad was such a wonderful person. I was never as lucky as Mom. I guess that was my problem. No man ever measured up to Dad."

His heart went out to her. He wanted to protect her. He reached out and grasped her hand to help her up. Enveloping her in his arms, he heard her gasp in surprise before she pulled away, and he let her go.

Instinct told him he had acted prematurely. He just hadn't been able to stop himself. She was like a wounded animal.

"I think it's time to head back." She had already reached Angel, and reins in hand, was swinging up into the saddle.

He castigated himself for coming on too fast. He would have to be more careful of her feelings. Fear of abuse and emotional pain was a powerful deterrent to letting another man into her heart. *I'll have to take a different tack.* He mounted his horse and they headed back to the gate. "Thank you for coming, and for lunch."

"You're welcome," she said in a flat voice, staring straight ahead.

"Can I see you again?" He hoped he hadn't scared her off.

Carla turned and looked at him. "I don't think that's a good idea. Somehow, I've given you the wrong impression. I'm not looking for a relationship."

Jason couldn't let her go under these circumstances. He'd never be able to regain the ground he'd lost. "I'm sorry if you feel I took advantage of you. That wasn't my intention. Please give me another chance—as a friend. I enjoy your company and riding together."

She sat astride Angel, but remained silent. The impatient mare pawed the ground.

Jason had another thought. "Do you like boats?"

Her expression changed, a smile filled her face and her eyes lit up. "Yes—I love boats. Boating and fishing were Dad's passions. The two of us spent time on the water whenever we could. I've loved being in or on water all my life. Randy and I spent a lot of weekends scuba diving in the summer. It was one of our favorite pastimes." That memory brought another wave of sadness that fell like a shadow across her face. She wrestled her emotions aside and concentrated on what Jason was saying.

"Well, I just happen to have a boat, nothing fancy, an eighteen-foot Reinell tri hull. Would you like to take it out next weekend?"

"I don't know." She looked away, felt her resolve faltering.

"Just as friends," he pleaded.

She swatted at a fly that landed on angel's neck. "That does sound like fun . . . I haven't been out on the water since Dad's stroke."

He could sense her resistance weakening. "A change would do you good."

"I suppose."

He looked so earnest she couldn't refuse.

"All right, I'll go." She gave him a weak smile. "I'll even make lunch. You supply the drinks."

"Good, I'll pick you up at nine."

"See you." She turned for home. *What is it about him? Why can't I just say no? I've got to work on that.*

# Chapter 16

Renfield stood at the white board writing down the list of items that had been found by the investigation team.

POND SITE:

    Cigarette butt – Freeman's DNA
    Gloves – Freeman's prints and DNA
    Tire tracks
    Footprints – Collier & Freeman

COLLIER FARM/PIT:

    Chevy Blazer – Tires match tracks
    Zip Ties

    Michael Freeman – waiting on DNA
        Pants – size 32,
        Tee-shirt –Med
        Tube socks
        Tennis shoes – size 9

    Greg Collier waiting on DNA

Tee-shirt – size 2x
Pants – size 44 Long
Black socks
Tennis shoes – size 13

Janice William  – purse and I.D.
Tim Sutton – bill-fold and I.D.
9mm Glock  Ballistics match
License plates– William's car
Mushroom collection bag – waiting on DNA
Plastic Bag – Blood – waiting on DNA

Chandry walked in and glanced over the list. "Looks like the loose ends are coming together."

"Yeah, as soon as we get the last DNA results we should be able to tie both suspects to the crime. The amount of circumstantial evidence is substantial. Still need to prove who pulled the trigger. Got to find a way to get Freeman to talk."

Renfield walked back to his desk and picked up the picture of Janice Williams. The dead woman still haunted his thoughts and he wouldn't give up working on the investigation.

Chandry paced back and forth, stopped to grind his shoe on an ant walking across the floor. "Freeman's a real dip stick. It seemed like he was ready to confess, but then changed his mind. How could he think he'd have a better chance with a jury? Don't know why he's so hard to convince."

"We'll have to go over everything again. Maybe there's something we've overlooked." Jim thumbed through one of the files.

The phone rang and interrupted his thoughts. "Detective Renfield."

"This is Paul Garner at the Kitsap County Jail."

"What's up Paul?"

"Your suspect, Michael Freeman, was stabbed last night."

Renfield jerked up straight. "What? You're kidding. How serious?"

"It wasn't lethal, but we had to send him to the hospital. He's there under guard. Had to go in for surgery, but he'll recover. They won't let anyone in to see him yet, but you may want to question him as soon as possible."

"Who did it?"

"Greg Collier. They got into some kind of altercation. We locked Collier in solitary. You might want to question him, too."

"This just might be our lucky break."

"That's a distinct possibility. Thought you'd want to know. I suggest you get over to the hospital as soon as they let visitors in to see Freeman."

"We're on it. Thanks for calling."

"No problem."

Renfield punched the off button. His eyes gleamed.

Chandry rolled his chair to Renfield's desk. "What was that about?"

Renfield filled him in and added, "This could be it. I'll bet Collier was trying to finish off Freeman to keep him from testifying." He closed the folders.

Chandry grinned. "This could be just the wedge we need to push Freeman over the top."

"Yeah, that's what I'm thinking. Damned lucky for us he survived. We'll have to be cautious. Freeman's got to be scared. We need to work that to our advantage." Renfield stood up and stretched, then carried the files over to the cabinet, dropped them inside the drawer and slammed it shut. "We'll know in a day or two. As soon as the doctor gives the okay we're going over there. Let's hope our bird starts to sing."

"Yeah, like a canary!" Chandry laughed and whistled a poor approximation of a bird song.

## Chapter 17

Jason had the boat trailer hooked up to his truck. An ice chest, soft drinks, water, a blanket and an extra pair of shoes were in the boat. In anticipation of a pleasant sunny day, he wore a pair of shorts underneath his jeans and an orange Tee-shirt under his navy blue sweatshirt. The sun was cooperating. An orange glow was already warming the air, evaporating the dew and transforming the morning chill. It was the beginning of a marvelous day.

Fishing poles, tackle box and life vests were always kept in the boat. He double-checked to be sure he had his fishing license. Fish didn't normally bite this late in the morning, but he so seldom took time to go fishing, he couldn't resist being prepared. A couple bottles of oil for the 65 horse Mercury outboard engine were ready; he just needed to stop at a nearby gas station to fill up the gas cans before he drove to Carla's house.

Carla dressed in a pair of lavender shorts with a matching cotton short-sleeved shirt. She pulled on a pair of loose-fitting jeans over her shorts and slipped a gray hoodie over her shirt, tied the laces on her white tennis shoes.

She was ready to go when the faded red pickup pulled up. She slung the strap of a large white shoulder-bag over her arm and picked up the plastic bag that held sandwiches, sliced carrots, apples and cookies.

She opened the front door, and Garth ran out, wagging his tail at the sight of Jason.

He reached for the bags. "Let me take those for you." He put their lunch inside the ice chest and set her shoulder bag in the front of the boat.

Garth watched her as she got into the truck and fastened her seat belt. "Sorry Garth, you'll have to stay home and guard the place." The dog turned around and lay down at the front door, chin resting on his paws.

Jason closed her door before getting in himself and drove off.

Carla shifted in her seat. "Where are we going?"

"I thought we'd go to Bremerton, launch at Evergreen Park, head south around Blake Island, then north along the west side of Bainbridge Island, under the Agate Pass Bridge and come down around the east side of Bainbridge. Is there a special place you'd like to go?"

"Not really. I'm happy to go anywhere. It's been a long time since I've been on the water. It'll be fun just to be out on the waves."

They arrived at the boat ramp, took their place behind three other boats lined up ahead, and waited their turn. Finally, the boat was unloaded and Carla waited on the dock while Jason parked the truck and trailer.

Jason walked down the dock. "Go ahead and get in." He motioned her toward the bow.

She stepped in over the side, worked her way back between the front-side windows and sat in the passenger seat on the port side. He climbed in, coiled the rope up front and pulled two lifejackets out of a cupboard in the bow. She slipped one over her head and fastened the straps. He put one on and took his place behind the steering wheel.

The Mercury engine fired right up. They backed away from the dock and headed toward deeper water.

Mount Rainier loomed in the background. Rising 14,411 feet above sea level, the snow-capped giant dwarfed the Cascade Range spreading north and south beneath it. There was very little wind and the sun's rays sparkled like diamonds across the glistening water.

Briny air filled their lungs as Jason pulled the throttle back and the boat picked up speed, sending a white foaming wake trailing behind them.

Carla reached into her bag and put on a pair of sunglasses and a purple University of Washington Huskies windbreaker.

They eased out into open water, passed under the Manette Bridge near Bremerton Naval Base, headed southwest across Sinclair Inlet and followed the coast along Orchard Point. Salty spray misted around them as the boat bounced across the blue-green waves.

The ferry, Kitsap, rounded the southern tip of Bainbridge Island as they entered the narrow passage at Manchester. Jason slowed down, turned the boat to head straight into the waves coming off the wake of the ferry making its run from Seattle to Bremerton. The water calmed and they left Manchester behind and sped to Blake Island.

With no bridge or ferry to the island, access was limited to boat traffic. That kept the 475 acre marine park with its 5 miles of shoreline isolated and free of normal beach crowds. Tour boats brought visitors to Tillicum village for traditional native style salmon dinners and dances.

A number of boats were anchored near the shore. Several people walked on the sandy beach. Jason steered away to avoid an oncoming sailboat.

They circled Blake Island and headed back past Manchester and Waterman. The Bremerton Naval shipyard came back into view, huge aircraft carriers in port dwarfing their small craft. They made a quick return into Sinclair Inlet, then continued north between the Kitsap Peninsula and Bainbridge Island.

Spacious elegant homes, some with very unique architecture, overlooked the water. Carla was fascinated by the magnificence of some of them. People were out on the beaches walking, beachcombing or perched on driftwood logs, taking advantage of the warm sunny weather.

Other boats passed by often and Jason had to slow down and turn into the waves as the wakes crossed their path. Boaters tended to be friendly and they waved back at the folks waving to them. Passing under the Agate Pass Bridge, they turned east around the north end of the island and traveled south down the east side.

Jason maneuvered the boat up to west side of Blakely Rock, a large conglomerate mound rising from the sandy bottom more than one hundred feet below in places, to a few feet above the surface off the southeast side of Bainbridge Island. A popular haunt of scuba divers, surrounded by swift currents, it provides an ideal habitat for the multitude of aquatic inhabitants that thrive among its many ledges, ridges and crevices.

Shutting down the motor, Jason allowed the boat to drift in near the rock. He didn't want to get too close and risk scraping the tri hull on the barnacle-covered stone. He tossed the anchor over the side. The boat rocked to the slurping rhythm of the lapping waves, pulling the anchor-line taught against the strong current. A group of harbor seals basking in the warm sunlight turned their heads and looked in their direction.

Jason stood up and stretched. "I thought this would be a good place to stop and have lunch."

"It's perfect here." She unzipped her windbreaker; it was warmer without wind blowing on them.

He opened the ice chest, and pulled out the bag containing their lunch and handed her a bottle of water, her preferred choice of drink, he remembered. He grabbed a root beer for himself.

It wasn't long before a flock of sea gulls abandoned their rocky perch and took to the air, surrounding the boat, swooping down with raucous cries imploring them to toss food. They broke off pieces of bread crust and hurled them into the air. The adept gulls caught them in flight. Carla's laughter, chimed across the water. They finished eating and put away the remains of lunch. The gulls continued to hover, or land in the water nearby, still hoping for another morsel.

"Can we stay a while?" Carla felt at peace, wanted to lie on the deck in the sun and watch the antics of the seals, birds and fish. All living creatures fascinated her. Observing them in their natural habitats was always a pleasure.

"We can stay as long as you want." Jason picked up a fishing pole and his tackle box and started sorting through lures. He fastened one onto the end of the line and cast it over the side of the boat.

Carla slipped out of her shoes, peeled off her jeans, windbreaker, and sweatshirt, and was comfortable in her cotton shirt and shorts. She applied sunblock to her exposed skin.

Jason took his eyes off the water and his pole to watch as she exposed parts of her body he had not yet seen. He followed her example and stripped down to his shorts and tee-shirt. "Could I use some of your lotion?"

"Sure." She handed him the bottle, then moved to the front of the boat and lay down with her head up to the edge so she could look over the bow into the water below.

Masses of bull kelp swayed with the waves. A seagull plucked a small kelp crab that ventured too close to the surface.

Carla remembered the last time she was here—diving with Randy—years ago. He had photographed ling cod, wolf eels, rockfish, sculpins and perch. A large Pacific octopus had attached the suckers of one tentacle to her arm when she reached her gloved hand into a crevice. So many creatures found sanctuary among the thousands of dark clefts below.

She closed her eyes and forced the memory of Randy from her mind, then opened her eyes and stared into the water. A butter yellow and white jellyfish was undulating a few feet away. A two-foot wide sun star and numerous orange and purple stars were visible just beneath the surface among flowery sea anemones, tentacles waving with the current. Half a dozen orange spotted nudibranches and a yellow lemon Dorid were visible near green-spined sea urchins. Sponges, mollusks and crabs added to the prolific gathering of creatures. Chitins, limpets, blue mussels, tube worms and barnacles clung tenaciously to rock in the wave-battered intertidal zone. Small fish darted within the tide pools. Every inch of submerged surface was home to some form of sea life.

Farther out, a seal poked its head above water and watched them for a minute before submerging. It resurfaced in the distance, then slipped underwater again and disappeared.

Jason pulled up his line and dropped it back down. Nothing was biting. His eyes focused on the long bare legs stretched out on the bow of the boat. They were firm and well-muscled. Her tight-fitting shorts accentuated the curvature of her butt. He willed his eyes back to the fishing pole, but they kept drifting over to her sexy body.

They stayed for about an hour before Carla said, "I think we'd better head back soon. I need to get home to feed the horses." She pulled on her jeans and slipped into the windbreaker. The quiet afternoon left her at peace. She was grateful for the lack of pressure to carry on a conversation. True to his word, he'd acted like nothing more than a friend. Strange, how the mere presence of Jason left her feeling content.

She was tying her shoelaces as Jason fastened down the fishing pole, returned the lure to its place in the tackle box and pulled up the anchor. He put on his jeans, socks and shoes and life-vest and took his seat at the helm. She sat across from him.

The engine roared into action, and he headed back to the boat ramp. They eased in to the dock. He threw fenders over, jumped out of the boat and wrapped the bow line around a cleat.

"Toss me the other line," he called out. He fastened it to cleat near the stern. "Wait here while I get the truck."

Carla watched him walk up the dock and then stared into the murky water. A dark brown kelp crab clung to the side of the float, clasping barnacles with its long, spindly legs. She bent down and moved her finger near the crustacean. He raised his claws in a threatening posture and she pulled her finger back.

She looked up when Jason backed the trailer down the ramp and into the water. Together they loaded the boat, climbed into the truck and headed home. They didn't say much during the ride. Both were relaxed and happy, talk was unnecessary.

The truck bounced down the gravel road to her driveway. Carla brushed hair away from her eyes and said, "That was really fun. Thank you for taking me."

"You're welcome. I love to go. Makes me realize I don't take enough time away from work." He was feeling optimistic. She seemed to be warming up to him. "We'll have to go again soon."

"I'd like that." Her smile was genuine.

Garth was there to greet them, his tail wagging furiously. Horses whinnied in the background, eager to be fed.

Jason carried Carla's bag into the house and set it down on the kitchen table. He took her hand in his and gently brought her to him. His arms wrapped around her and he kissed her lightly on the lips. Her arms clung to his neck, and she pulled him towards her. His lips had a faint taste of salt from the sea air. She felt his soft beard and liked how it tickled.

He ran his fingers down the length of her back. Light, feathery kisses sent shivers down her spine as he concentrated around the base of her ears and moved down the sides of her neck. His lips were soft and his tongue fluttered gently inside her mouth. Her body reacted involuntarily, sending heat waves from deep within her core, radiating outward, engulfing her.

Part of her began to panic. She didn't want this. Her brain was in conflict. Her mind signaled her to stop and send him away while her arms pulled him closer, encouraged him; her traitorous body succumbed.

She regained her self-control at last, grasped his hands in hers, and set them aside. Looking him in the eye she said, "Sorry, I just can't do this."

He pulled back with reluctance. "No need to apologize, I understand." He knew she'd been dealing with a lot of emotional baggage, but he'd misread her, believed she'd been ready to put all that aside. *God, I blew it again. How could I be so stupid?* He would have to give her more time. It took every ounce of his willpower to step away.

Jason regretted trying to push her too soon. He hadn't planned to, but he'd been so caught up in the emotion of the moment, he'd thrown caution to the wind, started something he would have to leave unfinished. His own pent-up needs would go unsatiated. He struggled with his emotions. "I'm sorry if I overstepped." Sorrier than she could imagine. "Thank you for a great time."

She looked at him unsmiling. "Thank you." It sounded hollow after their brief physical exchange.

"I'll call you soon." He turned and was out the door.

She stood there, rooted to the spot, watching him drive away, unmoving for a couple of minutes after he was gone. Inner turmoil wrenched her apart. He seemed too good to be true, but didn't they all at first? How long would it take before he showed his true colors? She just couldn't stand to go through that again. Her life felt like it was spiraling out of control. She had to keep him at a distance. He was getting too close. She couldn't go through another heartbreak.

Jason chastised himself all the way home. He knew by instinct she was emotionally fragile. He had enough of his own reasons to hesitate jumping into another relationship. She's like a wounded animal. He'd have to gain her trust. *How could I be such an idiot?* He had been so caught up in his feelings at the moment, helpless to resist, he'd made a mistake.

He would give her a break. Allow her some time to step back a bit, give her some space. He didn't want her to feel pressured. Perhaps the old saying, "Absence makes the heart grow fonder," would be the best tack to take at this point. He hoped so.

## Chapter 18

Renfield hung up the phone, "Come on, Rob, it's a go. The Doc's given his approval. We can get in to interview Freeman."

Chandry grabbed his jacket. "I'm right behind you."

Half an hour later they walked into the hospital. A guard was posted at the door of Freeman's room.

"Detective Renfield." Jim displayed his badge to the guard. "We're here to interview the prisoner."

Chandry flashed his badge as they went through the door.

Michael Freeman's appearance was altered from the last time they'd seen him. All color had drained from a face grimacing in pain. An IV line dripped clear fluid into his arm from a plastic bag hanging from a stainless steel post. A thin white blanket covered the bed and he was garbed in a pale blue hospital gown. His dirty blond hair hung in tangles, framing hollow pasty cheeks. Dilated pupils stared dully from narrow, glazed blue eyes.

Chandry's voice had a sarcastic edge. "You're not looking too well, Mick. Have a little disagreement with someone?" He pulled up a chair beside the bed and pretended to check the IV.

"It's nothin', man." Freeman flinched with pain as his taut lips uttered the words.

From the foot of the bed, Renfield noticed the labored breathing. "Really? I'd say a stab wound to the side, nicking a lung was pretty significant. It must have been just a warning. I figure if a man like Collier wanted to take you out, you wouldn't be lying here now. *I better be careful not to piss him off too much. He may not want to cooperate.*

"I ain't done nothin' to deserve this."

From the other side of the bed, Renfield pulled up another chair to get closer to Freeman's eye level. He leaned over. "We have witnesses. Some of your fellow prisoners saw and heard your little run-in. We know Collier told you to keep your mouth shut. Do you really want to get the death penalty protecting someone who doesn't care if you live or die? In fact, he would prefer you die. You're a pawn. One he can afford to lose. We can protect you. If you agree to testify, we can have him locked up in isolation. He won't be able to get to you anymore. We'll take the death penalty off the table for you. Such a deal." Renfield smiled.

Freeman lay quietly, finally spoke, his voice weak and raspy. "I don't want to go back to jail and have Greg kill me. You're right, this was a warning, but if the bastard changes his mind and comes for me again, I don't stand a chance." He coughed, then collapsed back. "Ohhhhh," he moaned. His eyes closed. He swallowed and lay quietly for a minute.

When he opened his eyes, he said, "If he's pissed off at me, my life won't be worth shit. I don't want to take the fall for what he did." He raised his head slightly. "What happens if I testify? How do I know he won't be able to get me? I'm doped up with painkillers. I don't remember what you said."

"Don't worry, Mick," Renfield replied. "You're worth more to us alive than dead. You can be sure you won't ever have to come into contact with Collier again. Do we have a deal?"

"Yeah . . . I guess so. But you make God damned sure you keep that son-of-a-bitch away from me."

Renfield assured him, "No problem. It's already in the works. We'll see you with your attorney next time to get things finalized and on the record. Hang tough."

"Yeah." Freeman groaned and collapsed back down flat on the bed. His face contorted as painful rasping coughs tore through his body. "Oooooooohhh." He closed his eyes and blinked back tears as he fought to breathe.

Renfield stood up. "We better leave. I'll send a nurse in to check on you."

Chandry followed him and paused at the door. "See you soon, Mick." He closed the door behind them. "Thank God. Collier did us a favor." He could barely contain his elation.

Renfield said, "He created the opposite effect of what he intended, but what a boon for us. Instead of shutting Freeman up, he pushed him over the edge to testify against him. We couldn't have planned it better." His voice took on a tone of concern. "Freeman sure looks like hell, though. Hope he pulls through okay. If he takes a turn for the worse and doesn't make it, we lose the advantage."

"Yeah, we need him to be in good enough shape to testify." Chandry pushed the button for the elevator.

They got in and doors closed. Renfield pushed the button for the first floor, pulled out a stick of gum, unwrapped it and popped it into his mouth. "Think I'll call Paula and tell her we're going out for dinner tonight. I feel like celebrating. There's a new restaurant she wants to check out. This seems like the perfect time."

They got out on the first floor and walked to the car. Chandry fastened his seatbelt. "I'm just going to go home, put my feet up and relax in front of the boob tube with a couple of beers. I haven't had much chance to wind down lately."

\* \* \*

The detectives sat across from Michael Freeman and his Kitsap County public defender Dale Tyson. The eyes of all the men turned to Kitsap County prosecutor Jennifer Lawrence.

She was seated at the head of the table. Soft brown curls framed her high cheekbones. The smile that lit up her face and sparkling pale blue eyes belied the tough character beneath the benign appearance.

She was prepared to wrap up this end of the case and move onto the charges against Gregory Collier. He was the more difficult challenge and she wanted to make sure she made no errors.

Lawrence's track record was nearly flawless. She was noted for her attention to detail; leaving nothing to chance. Juries could be a liability; she took every precaution to make sure she didn't lose cases by being unprepared or caught off guard. She believed in the law and the system in spite of instances when it didn't always seem to work. When it did fail, it hadn't been due to any failure on her part.

She had plenty of confidence in this investigation team. They were seasoned detectives with many years of experience among them and maintained the highest level of professional conduct under all circumstances. She was fairly unconcerned about the possibility of any problems cropping up. "In addition to the video camera, a separate sound recorder will be used to record our conversation. Gentlemen, shall we begin?"

Renfield turned on the recorder.

Dale Tyson spoke up. "My client is concerned for his safety and feels he is a victim in this situation, too. Collier was a threat to him as well as the victims. It was never his desire to have those people killed. He was an unwilling accomplice in the cover-up, and he has maintained his innocence as far as the actual homicides are concerned."

The prosecutor looked the PD in the eye, "Mr. Tyson, your client has already agreed to testify against Collier in exchange for a reduction in sentence. I'm willing to take the death penalty off the table in his case and charge him as an accessory to murder with sentence of ten to fourteen years. Mr. Freeman is far from a model citizen. He participated in the murders and did not come forward to report them."

Freeman slouched down in his chair, clenched his teeth as a bolt of pain wracked his chest. Bandages beneath the orange prison coveralls caused the fabric to pull too snugly across his injury. His face was flushed. "You people are talkin' about me like I'm not even here. There's no way I'm gettin' out of this shit. I just wanna get this over with. Said I'd tell ya."

"Are you ready to give an account of what happened, Mr. Freeman?" Lawrence said.

"Yeah." He drummed his fingers on the table. "I'm ready."

She looked at the attorney. "Do you have any problem with that, Mr. Tyson?"

"No. It's up to my client."

She began the interrogation. "Okay, Mr. Freeman, start at the beginning and tell us exactly what happened to the victims."

He stared at her red polished manicured nails. "I was out back checkin' on the weed."

"You are referring to marijuana growing at the back of the property?"

Freeman picked at a scab on his arm left by the IV. He closed his eyes for a few seconds, swallowed and took a deep breath. "Yeah, I heard voices way out back."

"Were they men or women?" She reached up and brushed a curl away from her cheek.

His right eye started to twitch. "A man and a woman."

"Could you hear what they were saying?"

"No." He fought to stifle a cough, but was unable to prevent the irritation. He pressed his arms to his chest and hunched over as the familiar agonizing waves burned through his side. "Can I have somethin' to drink?" he croaked.

Chandry got up. "I'll get you some water. Anyone else want any?"

"I'd like a drink," Lawrence said.

Renfield shook his head, "No, thanks."

Tyson held up a tall mug. "Brought my own, thanks."

Chandry left the room. The prosecutor sat in silence and studied the man in front of her.

Freeman was slumped in the chair, eyes closed. His breaths were short, raspy between clenched teeth. They sat in silence until the door opened and Chandry walked in carrying two bottles of water. He handed one to Lawrence.

She smiled. "Thank you." Opened the bottle and took a sip.

He loosened the cap on the other and placed it in front of Freeman.

"Thanks," the prisoner mumbled. He finished unscrewing the cap, drank slowly, wiped his hand across his lips.

"You're welcome." Chandry sat down next to his partner. "How's it going?" He took his seat.

Renfield looked at Freeman, and back to Chandry. "We were waiting for you."

The DA asked, "Mr. Freeman, are you ready to continue?"

"Yeah."

She asked, "What did you do after you heard voices?"

"I ran back to the garage—told Greg."

"What happened after that?"

He looked away then down at the floor. His hands clenched and unclenched. At last he spoke. "Greg grabbed some zip-ties and rubber gloves, and stuffed them in his pocket. He checked the gun he always carried and made sure it had a full clip—told me to follow."

She leaned forward and looked him in the eye. "Did anyone else go with you?"

He shook his head slowly. "No."

"What happened next?"

"We was bein' real quiet. Stopped out in the weed to listen. We heard voices, but I couldn't hear what they was sayin'. Greg pulled out his gun an' snuck up on 'em."

Jennifer raised an eyebrow. "Where were you when Greg pulled his gun on the victims?"

"Behind, 'bout ten feet back. I didn't have no gun."

"What happened next?"

"Greg took the zip-ties out of his pocket, and gave 'em to me. He told 'em to get their hands behind their backs, and told me to fasten 'em."

"Did you do that?"

His eye started twitching again. He looked away, "Uh—yeah—the lady started cryin'. "Greg asked what they was doin' there. The guy said, 'Hey, don't kill us, man. We're just pickin' mushrooms.' He said they didn't know our place was there. Said they wouldn't tell anybody."

He exhaled loudly and rubbed his hands together. He picked up the bottle and took a drink.

Jennifer took a sip while she waited for him to resume, but he set his bottle down and just stared into space.

"So, what happened next?"

"Greg asked 'em where they came from. They pointed to the road. He told 'em to walk back where they came from.

"I thought he was gonna let 'em go. The lady was out in front. The man was behind her. Greg walked behind the man and kept the gun pointed at his back. He told me to come, too. I was last. The guy kept tellin' Greg not to shoot 'em. The lady cried all the way." Freeman coughed and clasped his arms to his sides. He inhaled, took a drink, then ran his tongue around his lips and swallowed.

Jennifer allowed time for him to recover, then asked, "Are you ready to continue?"

Freeman looked at his attorney, and rubbed his fingers across his chest. The pain from the wound was getting worse the longer he sat there. He winced as he spoke. "How long is this gonna take?"

Renfield answered, "That all depends on you. Keep talking and it'll get over sooner."

"We walked to where we could see the car. Greg asked if that was their car. The guy said 'Yeah.' Greg told 'em to 'stop right there.' He asked the guy where his keys was. He told Greg they was in his pocket.

"Greg stuck the gun up to the guy's head and shot him. The lady started screaming. He grabbed her and shot her in the head. He took the keys out of the guy's pocket. He told me to drag the bodies to the car and put them in the back seat."

He ground his teeth and rubbed his fingers across his chin. His eyes teared up, looked into hers. "I told him, I didn't wanna touch dead bodies. He said, 'Tough shit. Get 'em over to the car, asshole.' I didn't wanna end up dead, so I did what he said."

He took another drink. His fingers curled around the bottle and crumpled the plastic. Water spurted out the top and spilled onto the table. He put the cap back on, then ran his fingers through the water, smearing it across the table.

Jennifer waited silently, giving him time to gather his thoughts. After a couple of minutes she spoke. "What exactly did you do next?"

"Greg gave me a pair of gloves. I put 'em on. I grabbed the lady by the waist and drug her to the car. Then he gave me the keys. I opened the car doors and pushed her onto the back seat. I went back and drug the man the same way. I put him in next to the lady." His shoulders sagged as he looked around the room, "I really didn't want to do it. I didn't have a choice. I'd a been as dead as they were." A tear rolled down his cheek. He brushed it away with his hands.

Lawrence spoke softly, "How did you get rid of the bodies?"

"Greg told me to get in the car and wait. He walked back to the farm to get the Blazer then drove back to where I was waitin'. He told me to give him her purse and the man's wallet and said to drive their car and follow him. We drove to the tree farm."

"You are referring to the Northwest Tree Farm?" she asked.

"Yeah, Greg drove off the road and through the brush. He stopped near the pond. I stopped next to him. Greg got out and told me to drive back from the edge, head it at the pond and get out. He took off the license plates and put 'em in the Blazer."

She asked, "How did you get the car into the pond?"

"Greg told me to put it in neutral. He went and got a big stick. I smoked a cigarette till he got back. He pinned the gas pedal to the floor. He had me lean in and start the car, shift into drive, and then slam the door and jump away. I done it just like he said. Worked slicker'n shit. I took off the gloves and hid 'm in a bush and walked back to the truck; then we took off. I never thought no one would find 'em in there."

She felt confident this testimony would convict Collier. "Do you have anything else to add?"

He leaned back in the chair and sighed. "Nope—that's it."

"You'll be willing to testify to all of these facts in a court of law as you related them to us here?"

He nodded his head, "Yeah, you make sure you keep Greg away from me. When he finds out I ratted him out, I'll be dead meat if he gets to me."

Renfield smiled, "Don't worry, Mick. It's important to us to keep you alive. As long as you cooperate, you can be sure Collier won't get anywhere near you."

The DA spoke to the client's attorney, "Mr. Tyson, I believe we are in agreement."

"Yes. My client will plead guilty to accessory to murder, and will testify against Collier in exchange for fourteen years and removal of the death penalty."

Renfield stepped back from his chair and turned off the recorder. "I'll have all the paperwork typed up for signatures before we see you in court."

- Jennifer Lawrence said, "Perfect. It looks like we'll be getting this wrapped up soon. I'll have my paralegal prepare the court documents."

Chandry breathed a sigh of relief. He was grinning from ear to ear.

Renfield said, "It won't take much time to get Freeman's case tied up, then we can concentrate on Collier. At least we'll have his hearing out of the way soon, then it's just a matter of waiting for Collier's court date. He felt like a huge weight had just been lifted off his shoulders.

## Chapter 19

Jason was checking property lines, making sure no one had trespassed. He walked along the line inspecting trees as he went. It was methodical work gave his mind plenty of time to wander. The trees were in very good condition. The needles were deep green, not yellow or brown, free of parasites, not brittle and dry.

He chastised himself over the move he'd put on Carla. He knew it was too soon, but his body had overridden his brain. Every time he looked at her, he forced himself to keep a tight rein on his emotions. She brought out feelings he'd been afraid to feel for a long time. He envisioned her full curves, soft skin and inviting lips, and imagined his hands roaming over her oh-so-desirable body. He forced the vision from his thoughts. He would have to be patient if he wanted to win Carla's heart.

He believed she would be worth the wait if he could just manage to keep his physical desires in check. *If she'll see me again. I'll have to do better.*

Francine left years ago, but sometimes he felt like it was only yesterday. They say time heals a broken heart, but that wasn't exactly true. Part of his heart would always be with Francine.

Funny how life seemed to cycle. A heart would get hurt, but always seemed ready to open up to get hurt again. He told himself he would never let another woman into his life. *I'm getting too old for this, getting used to living alone.* Now his heart was doing it again, getting him into trouble.

He had worked his way down the length of the property across the backside, and was just heading back up front when he heard a feeble, "Meow."

He looked in the direction of the sound and didn't see anything but endless rows of evergreens.

"Meow."

There it was again. His eyes searched in the direction of the sound.

"Meow—meow."

Finally he saw it, a tiny orange ball of fluff. He walked over and picked it up. *Oh, great. What am I going to do with you?*

The kitten's long fur was matted and imbedded with burrs, thorns, and twigs. The scrawny creature started to purr as soon as it settled into Jason's arms. He started back to his truck when he heard another.

"Meow."

*Oh, no—not another one.* More searching and he spotted not one, but two more kittens, a cream colored long-hair and a short-haired tabby huddled together under a Douglas fir.

*Well, this is just wonderful. I hope there aren't any more.* He was having difficulty hanging on to all of them. They were not content to sit still and were trying to climb up his sleeves, burying sharp, tiny claws in the flesh of his arms. "What am I going to do with you guys?" He carried them back to his truck and deposited the squirming kittens on the seat.

He left the windows open just a crack and left the kittens while he went back to search for more. As far as he could tell, there weren't any others. He heard their ear-piercing yowling cries as he approached his pickup.

Jason got in and pulled the door shut before they could escape. He had to keep pulling them off his clothes as he drove. They were not cooperating at all, and crawled over him, getting down near his feet and the pedals. *Thank God I'm close to home.* It was still the middle of the day. The horses weren't used to seeing him so early. Ranger and Teasel nickered at the possibility of an early meal.

Jason set the kittens on a bale of straw while he searched for a shallow pan and filled it with water. They drank most of the water and then resumed their meowing chorus.

"I bet you guys are really hungry. I better get you something to eat." He left them there, closed the door behind him and walked to the house. A few minutes later he came back with a milk-filled cereal bowl. They greedily lapped up milk. Drops of white liquid adhered to the fur on their faces. "You'll have to stay here while I go get you some food and supplies."

Jason walked into the store and went to the pet section. He put kitty litter, a litter box, a bag of kitten food and dishes into his cart. He recognized two men standing in front of him in the check-out line. "Remember me? Jason Gerard."

"You're the tree patrolman who discovered the bodies in the pond." Renfield extended his hand. Chandry nodded.

Jason set his items on the conveyor belt. "How's the investigation going? I haven't heard from you. Been wondering."

Renfield laid a ten dollar bill on the counter. The cashier bagged a couple bottles of flavored water and handed him the change. He turned back and looked at Jason. "As a matter of fact, it's going real well. We're getting close to wrapping it up. You'll be contacted to testify when it goes to trial."

"Of course, I'll be there."

Chandry noticed Jason's items. "Get a new cat?"

Jason shrugged his shoulders and smiled. "Just found three kittens on the tree farm. People are always dumping animals." He shook his head and sighed. "Didn't have the heart to drop them off at Animal Control, so here I am."

Chandry set a bottle of juice on the counter and paid the clerk. "At least you haven't run into any more corpses."

"Hope I never find another. I still have nightmares over the last ones."

"It's hard to get used to." Renfield waved as the detectives walked out. "Take care."

Jason got home and the kittens were settled around the bowls waiting to eat. He'd have to clean them up, but he'd do that another day. He gave them some food and stood there watching them eat. *Poor things were starving.* He unfolded an old blanket and laid it on a bail of straw.

Now, it was time to take care of the horses. He mucked out the stalls and fed them. He checked on the kittens before leaving the barn. They were curled up together asleep on the blanket

It was getting too late to go back to work. He'd have an early dinner. He washed up, and prepared some hamburger for a meatloaf, and put the meat and a potato in the oven.

He picked up the remote, settled onto the couch, turned on the TV and flipped through channels. Local weather was on and the forecast was cloudy with a chance of light rain, but it will clear up by Saturday.

The newscaster came back and talked about the murders of Tim Sutton and Janice Williams. Photographs of the victims were shown, and then members of their families spoke to a reporter, relieved that one of the killers had confessed. Next, the camera switched to Freeman, a thin blonde man in orange prison garb restrained with handcuffs. He stood before a judge and entered a plea of guilty as an accomplice to murder.

*That's good news. The families will at least be able to have some closure. The detectives did a great job. The criminals in this case will be prosecuted and off the street.* Jason was glad he'd been able to play a role in solving the case. *If I hadn't found the car, the crime might never have been solved.*

He thought back to that day. The first time he met Carla. Those long slender legs, full round breasts, and dark mysterious eyes. He couldn't get her out of his mind. Everything seemed to bring his thoughts back to her. No matter how hard he tried, he just couldn't forget the troubled woman. There was a warm, compassionate, loving, kindhearted person behind the emotional obstacles. If only he could be patient long enough to break through the psychological barricade, he'd be able to reach her.

He had his own fears to overcome. How could he blame her for being leery? He'd have to win her trust; prove he wasn't another bad guy unworthy of her love.

He was in a muddle, not sure how to proceed. A new thought entered his mind. *Perhaps a public setting would help put her at ease. I'll call her tomorrow and invite her to lunch.*

He ate in front of the TV, then went to bed early. Visions of her on her horse galloping through evergreens pervaded his dreams.

## Chapter 20

Carla sat at her desk looking over a file for one of her accounts. Jasmine, informed her she had a call.

Still looking at the file, she picked up the phone. "Hello?"

"Hi, Carla, it's Jason."

She paused and swallowed; a lump seemed to form in her throat. "Jason—how are you?"

"Fine, thanks, how about you?"

"I've been busy."

"Are you too busy to take time off for lunch?"

"Today?" Her fingers tightened on the phone.

"If that works." He didn't want her to have time to refuse.

"Uhh—I guess so."

His heart was pounding. "What time?"

"I take a lunch break at eleven-thirty."

"Good, I'll pick you up."

"I'll be ready."

"See you then."

She set the phone down and leaned back in her chair. His call caught her off guard and she didn't have time to come up with an excuse. She struggled to concentrate on the numbers before her. Her thoughts kept drifting to the last time she saw him. He'd made a pass at her. She'd encouraged him at first, changed her mind and sent him away.

She hadn't heard from him since, that was three weeks ago. *Thought I'd seen the last of him; apparently not.* What would he expect of her? She wasn't ready to deal with a man. Maybe she never would be. Carla struggled to concentrate on the numbers on the computer screen in front of her.

She was financially independent and very capable of taking care of herself. He was persistent, seemed determined to tear down her defenses. She was faced with a dilemma. *Should I take a chance? He could turn out to be Mr. Right. Or should I continue to remain alone and avoid the risk of being hurt again?*

Her emotional wrestling match continued; she was unsure of the outcome.

She stared at the spreadsheet on the screen, but all she saw was Jason. *Good thing it's not tax time.* She glanced at her watch: 11:20. The morning was shot, nothing got done.

Carla rose from her desk and stopped by the reception area. "Jasmine, I have a lunch appointment, so I'll be in the restroom for a few minutes getting ready." She wanted to run a brush through her hair and touch up her make-up.

Jason arrived at Carla's office and walked over to the receptionist. "I'm Jason Gerard here to see Carla Summers."

The young black-haired Amer-Asian woman seated behind the desk smiled; her dark eyes opened wide as he came in. "Carla will be out shortly. Would you like to have a seat?"

"Thanks." He sat in an oak chair and looked at several lithographs of Northwest Native American art adorning the walls: killer whales, bald eagles, herons and salmon.

The heavy oak door opened and Carla entered the room. He noticed her calf-length flowered skirt, cream-colored blouse and gray jacket. He felt underdressed in his pale green short-leaved shirt, jeans and ball cap.

"Hi, Jason, have you been waiting long?"

"No, just a few minutes."

"This is my secretary Jasmine. Jasmine, this is Jason."

"Hello, Jasmine. It's a pleasure to meet you." He smiled warmly.

"It's nice to meet you, Jason." She smiled back.

"Jasmine, I'll be out for a while. If anyone needs to speak to me, please tell them I'll be back by two."

"Yes, I'll do that. Have a nice lunch."

Jason reached the door and held it open for Carla. "Where are you parked?" She looked for the beat-up red pickup.

"Right over here." He walked over to a dark blue older Chevy Malibu, opened the passenger door, waited for her to get in and closed the door.

He slid in and fastened his seat belt. "Is there some place special you'd like to go?"

"There's a Chinese place close by on the bay."

"I know the place. Food's good there."

"Yes, it is." She looked out her window to avoid his eyes.

The restaurant was about five minutes away. The parking lot was full. He drove around to find a space. He got out and locked his door, but she was out of the car before he reached her side.

He held the restaurant door for her as they went in, took off his hat and smoothed his hair. A hostess seated them at a booth and placed menus on the table. Ginger-spiced aromas teased their senses as they looked over the menu and made their selections.

The waitress took their order and returned with a pot of tea. They both asked for chopsticks, waited for their meal. They sat in silence, eyes roaming gold-framed Chinese landscapes adorning the red walls. Wonton soup came promptly and they started to eat.

The waitress returned and placed steaming platters heaped with food in front of them. They helped themselves, filling their plates with aromatic, tantalizing foods.

Jason contemplated how to break the silence and engage her in a non-threatening conversation. He didn't want to blow this opportunity to make progress, even if it came in the tiniest, almost imperceptible increments. He felt optimistic she had agreed to meet for lunch and not decided against further contact with him. But he wanted to be sure he didn't frighten her off.

He picked a safe topic. "How's your colt doing?"

Her dark eyes lit up. "He's doing great. I started putting a blanket on his back, and he lets me rub him down. He loves to have his neck scratched. I can watch him for hours . . ." She was laughing, relaxed and talking animatedly without reservation. As long as the conversation was about horses, she felt comfortable, in control.

He decided to turn the conversation to a more personal level. "I've been such a work-a-holic; I haven't had much time for my horses. That was one of Francine's complaints. I wasn't home enough. Something always seemed to come up at work." He took a sip of tea.

Carla looked up from her plate and into his eyes as he spoke.

"I kept up the yard, did repairs and took care of any heavy chores that needed to be done for the horses and farm. I even helped her with housework and took care of the kids when I could. I'm a pretty good chef, and we used to cook together sometimes. I never really understood what went wrong." Jason lowered his eyes and pushed a shrimp around in a circle with his chopsticks.

Carla picked up an egg roll, but paused and held it above her plate. "Did you communicate with her? Try to find out what the problem was?"

"I did. We even tried counseling for a while. It was frustrating. She was so needy and I couldn't always be there."

"That was all? How could any woman end a marriage for so little reason? Did you argue or fight a lot?"

"Not really. We had some disagreements on occasion, but I never considered them to be anything major. Apparently, she did. I guess I'm guilty of not communicating enough. I failed her and she just wanted to be done with me.

I loved Francine. In a way I still do. You never really stop loving someone you gave your heart to, do you? A broken heart heals; like every wound, there's a scar, a memory, but it heals."

"I don't know. My scars run too deep." She looked at the egg roll she'd been holding in her chop sticks and took a bite and crunched. "I gave a hundred percent in my relationships; put my heart and soul into them. When Randy got into drugs, he stopped caring about me; about our life together. All he thought about was getting high and how to buy more drugs. Nothing I did or said could change that. It broke my heart to see the man I loved degenerate into an empty shell." She stared at her plate, picked up her napkin, dabbed her eyes and then twisted the napkin between her fingers.

Carla placed the crumpled paper beside her plate and took a sip of tea. I sigh escaped her lips and she smiled narrowly. "You'd think after thirteen years, I'd be over it."

His gaze met her eyes and he shook his head slowly. "No, you can't forget the heartache, but you do need to put it behind you and move on. You just haven't found the right man."

"Hmmmm." Carla picked up her chop sticks and ate a bit of chow mien. She continued eating without saying anything about his comment.

They ate in silence for a while. Jason was at a loss for words. *I've done it again, pushed her too far. The barriers are up again.* "Give me a chance. I'm a good guy. I won't hurt you. You deserve to be happy. Everyone needs love and companionship, don't they?"

"I used to believe that." She looked away, her eyes focused on misty hills overlooking a winding river hanging on the wall on other side of the room.

He reached across the table, picked up her hand and clasped it between both of his. "Give me the opportunity to change your mind."

Carla met his gaze, but didn't say anything for a minute. "I'll think about it. You can't expect me to trust you right away. "So do I, you aren't the Lone Ranger. I have plenty of negative baggage to get over myself."

"I know. It's selfish of me to think I'm the only one who's been hurt." They locked eyes.

"Carla, I don't believe you're selfish. I think you've become so wrapped up in your emotions, you haven't realized men can go through the same things." He exhaled a deep breath. "There are plenty of dysfunctional women out there." His eyes looked down at his plate his expression grew sad "Believe me, I know. I don't want to be hurt again either."

"Guess I hadn't thought about that, but I should have. I'm sorry."

He let go of her hand and picked up his chopsticks. "We better finish lunch so you're not late for your appointment."

"Yes." She popped a shrimp into her mouth.

They finished eating and continued talking, making idle conversation. The waitress brought fortune cookies along with the bill. Carla opened hers and read, "A change for the better in your future."

"See? I'm in your future." He laughed and she did too.

"I love to hear you laugh." He read his fortune, "You will be rewarded for your efforts." He raised his eyebrows and flashed a smile before he ate his cookie.

"So, will you give me a chance?" He reached out and squeezed her hand.

"Yes—I will." A beautiful smile formed on her lips.

They drove in silence back to the office. He walked her to the door and they paused outside. He gave her a hug. "Can I see you Friday night?"

Out of habit, she hesitated, but then she checked herself and said, "Yes—you can."

"Good. I'll pick you up at six. I'll make dinner for you this time. The weather's supposed to clear up, so we'll have a barbecue."

"That sounds nice. What would you like me to bring?"

"Why don't you bring some vegetables and I'll get the meat. I'll take care of all the preparation. I'd get everything, but you grow better vegetables than they sell at the store and I know how you feel about produce." He winked.

"I'll be ready with my vegetables."

"Good, I'll see you then."

"Thank you for lunch."

"You're welcome." He held the door as she walked in. He returned to his car with a new feeling of confidence.

"How was lunch?" Jasmine greeted Carla as she walked in.

"It was very good."

Jasmine grinned. "I wasn't asking about the food. He seems like a nice man."

"Yes, he does, doesn't he?" Her eyes flashed. "I'll be in my office."

She remembered how happy she and Randy were before he got mixed up with drugs. *Maybe I could be happy again.* She sat down and touched the mouse

## Chapter 21

"How does your client plead to the charge of Accessory to Murder?" The judge focused on the public defender Dale Tyson and the handcuffed prisoner sitting beside him.

Tyson replied. "Guilty."

Family members and friends of Tim Sutton and Janice Williams filled the crowded courtroom. A collective sigh of relief and subdued sobbing was audible as Michael Freeman's plea was entered.

The prisoner sat in silence as, one by one; family members voiced their grievances against him, gave poignant remarks in memory of the victims, and verbalized their anger and grief.

After the final speaker was finished, Michael Freeman rose and stood with head bowed and faced to the angry, grieving crowd.

Tears flowed freely from the dull blue eyes as he spoke. "I am truly sorry for the pain I caused. Didn't want nothin' to do with killin'. I didn't know what to do. Knew it was wrong. I wish I'd done somethin' to stop it. I'm sorry."

The judge adjourned the hearing and guards took Freeman back to jail. He was headed to prison. He would be back for sentencing and then again to testify in court against Greg Collier.

Other members of the original bust faced various theft and drug charges, but murder charges were only being brought against Collier.

\* \* \*

A week later, Friends and family members of the victims gathered outside the courtroom after sentencing to console one another and gather their composure. Several reporters from local news stations were there to record reactions to the judge's decision.

"How do you feel about the sentence of ten years, 4 months in this case?" A young woman from Channel 4 held out a microphone to the tearful sister of Janice Williams.

"I know Michael Freeman wasn't the one who pulled the trigger, but it was awful what they did. He did show remorse and he is willing to testify against Collier. I want Collier to die. They murdered my sister and her fiancé for no reason. Nothing will bring Jan or Tim back. I can't forgive them." She turned away and dabbed her eyes with a damp hanky.

Tim Sutton's father spoke next. "It's all the drug people. They don't care about anyone, just feeding their habit. Most of the crimes in our area are tied to them. Cops need to bust them all and put them away. I don't pity any of the creeps. Criminals destroy lives of innocent people, get out, and do it again. I wish judges and courts would be harder on the crooks. We need to stop the revolving door of our justice system. I want Greg Collier to die for what he did to my son and to Jan. They were good people and didn't deserve to die." He stepped back; no longer able to prevent the flow of tears that rolled down his weathered, deep-creased face.

County prosecutor Jennifer Lawrence started down the courthouse steps.

"How is the case against Greg Collier coming? Will you be seeking the death penalty?" A reporter held a microphone for her to speak.

"The Collier case is coming together. That's all I'm willing to say at this time." She continued down the steps.

Chandry and Renfield crossed the parking lot.

Renfield said, "One down, one to go."

Chandry kicked a stone across the concrete. "I wish Freeman would get a longer term. He's a dirt bag who's going to get off way too easy."

"Yeah, but then we'd have a tough time proving Collier pulled the trigger. Besides, Freeman's guilty plea spared the family the trauma of a second jury trial. He'll get ten years and we'll get Collier."

"True, those people have been through hell."

Renfield stopped and picked up a soda can someone had tossed beside the sidewalk. "Boy, some slob dropped their litter right beside the courthouse."

Chandry laughed. "Yeah, and we're here to clean up after another schmuck."

"Well, let's get back to work and take care of Collier." Renfield crushed the can in his hand. "I want to make sure that bastard never sets foot out of prison."

## Chapter 22

Jason took off from work early and went to the grocery store to pick up two T-bone steaks and a bottle of wine. He wanted to make sure he had everything ready. He got home, cleaned the grill, and finished the rest of his preparations. At 5:45 he headed over to pick up Carla.

Garth started barking when the car drove up. Carla opened the door and looked out to see the blue Malibu. Garth stood his ground, hackles up, until the door opened and he recognized Jason. Canine whines, tail-wagging, and an enthusiastic tongue replaced the aggressive bark.

"You know a friend when you see one, don't you, buddy?" Jason handed him a dog biscuit, which disappeared in a few quick crunches, then his hands found the base of the big dog's ears. Garth moaned in pleasure and the long muzzle snuggled against his leg.

Jason grinned at the dog. *If only Carla was as willing to accept me as you are.*

"He certainly thinks you're wonderful." Carla's eyes ran him up and down; baseball cap with the fringe of brown hair extending below, dark brown Tee-shirt and beige shorts. She couldn't help but notice his firm muscular legs.

"He knows a good man when he sees one. You could learn a lesson from your dog." He stopped rubbing the dog, looked up with a wink and flashed a smile.

"Really?" Her hands were on her hips and her voice displayed a hint of sarcasm, but the smile told him she had taken his comment with a degree of humor.

"You look terrific." His eyes traveled down the tight blue jeans and then up to the well-filled plaid cotton shirt. "Can I have a hug?"

"I suppose."

He stopped rubbing the dog and moved to encompass her with his arms. "Ooh, you feel so good." He was hesitant to let her go. "I guess we better get going if we want to eat before too long. Are you ready?"

"Yes. I'll get the veggies. It'll just take a minute." She disappeared into the house and came out with a large plastic bowl.

"Let me take that." He glanced in before placing it in the back of the car. "You've got peaches in there."

"Right off the tree. I thought you'd like them."

She was already seated by the time he got back to her door, but he closed it for her. Garth followed them to the end of the drive before he turned back to the house.

Jason lived a couple of miles away, down a back road. Wheels ground on crushed rock as he pulled up and parked in front of the small house. "It needs paint."

"I would say so!" Her brows furrowed as her eyes glimpsed the weathered boards showing through peeling gray paint.

"I spend so much time at work; I don't get much time to get things done at home."

A procession of carpenter ants scurried along a rotting pole. "Looks like your fence could use a few new rails, that is, unless you're growing moss intentionally."

"Ha ha, very funny. No, it's just one more thing I haven't had time to do."

She nodded her head. "I can see that."

"I haven't been home much." He got out and came around to open her door.

"Maybe you don't have time to see me?" She teased as she got out.

He wrapped his arms around her. "I'll make time for you." His lips found hers and they stood there caught up in the moment.

She pulled back. "If we don't get dinner on soon we won't be eating tonight."

"Right." He took the vegetables and they walked to the house.

"I'll make the salad." She followed him into the kitchen

"I want to do everything so you can relax. Why don't you sit down?"

"I'd like to take a walk down to the barn so I can see your horses."

"I'll work on dinner." He took a knife from a drawer, picked up a cucumber and began to slice.

She slid open the barn door and walked inside. A kitten jumped down off a bale of hay, followed by its siblings.

"Ouch!" Carla plucked a tiny warm body from her pant leg where it climbed up. She held the furry creature in front of her face. "You are going to have to learn to stay on the ground." She kept it in her arms stroking the orange fur. The other two meowed then the tabby jumped up and attached itself to her leg. She picked it off, and now had two of them in her arms.

"All right, that's enough." She set them back down and stroked the cream one so it wouldn't feel left out. They purred, rubbed against her legs. She had to be careful not to step on them as she walked to the nearest stall and peered in. Ranger glanced up from his rack of hay. The familiar buckskin was intent on the food before him, so he didn't pay her much notice. "You're going to ignore me. I see; you'd rather eat."

The black and white paint in the neighboring stall was equally busy with the hay in front of her, but she eyed the stranger briefly before she took another mouthful.

Carla walked through the barn, inspected the stacks of hay and checked out the tack room before returning to the door. She spent more time petting and talking to the kittens before going outside. She was careful to keep them in the barn as she slid the door closed.

Back at the house she found Jason out back. "I didn't know you had cats."

"I didn't until this week. I found them on the tree farm. Someone abandoned them. They were starving and tangled in burrs. I'm not a cat person, but I couldn't leave them."

"Two of them climbed up my leg." She laughed, rubbed her shin.

"Sorry, I forgot to warn you." He placed the steaks on the grill.

She looked across the tall grass and weeds spreading across the yard. "That's okay."

"Domestic animals are dependent upon their owners to take care of them. It makes me angry to see how cruel or just plain stupid some people are—how they treat their pets. They don't neuter their dogs or cats.

Unwanted puppies or kittens are just dumped in the woods. They can't survive on their own; it just doesn't happen. They face a slow certain death. By the time I find them, it's usually too late, especially the young ones." He stared at smoke wafting up from the sizzling coals. "These kittens were fortunate I found them in time."

"You are a softy, aren't you—a very compassionate person." She smiled and laid her hand on his arm.

"That's true. I hate to see suffering, animals or people. I've been in a war. It's one thing to destroy an enemy who's trying to kill you. It's another thing to see an innocent animal or person, particularly a baby or young child suffer. It's so senseless. I never have been able to stomach that." He exhaled with a deep sigh, and then looked at his watch, timing the meat.

"Me either. What will you do with the kittens?" Her stomach growled as the aroma of grilling meat filled her nostrils.

"I'll keep them. They can live in the barn. Maybe they'll keep the rats and mice out. They won't be too much trouble out there. At least they'll have a home." He turned the steaks.

"That's good. How's dinner coming? Do you need help?"

"No, I've got everything under control. How do you like it?"

"Medium rare."

He pressed a finger onto the meat. "It's almost done. Have a seat." He gestured toward the picnic table where a tempting salad was centered on a red and white-checked vinyl table cloth.

She sat down and poured them each a glass of wine. She sipped slowly as he tended the meat. He moved a steak to a plate and set it on the table in front of her, then served himself. They sat in the shade of a giant red cedar.

Carla cut off a piece of meat and chewed slowly. "The steak is perfect; my compliments to the chef." Her lips parted in a smile that filled her face and lit her eyes.

A man taking care of her was an unfamiliar luxury. She was curious about this man who seemed determined to insinuate himself into her life. "How did you end up working for Northwest Tree Farm?"

"I worked for them off and on part-time, mostly during the busy Christmas season. After I retired from the Army, I was looking for a change of pace. When Ray offered me the tree patrolman position, I jumped at the chance. I get to work out in nature, no irritating deadlines or major pressures." His fingers stroked his beard. "It suits my personality." He lifted a forkful of salad into his mouth. "Your fresh vegetables are delicious."

They ate without hurrying, chatting about nothing in particular. Following the main course, they sipped wine and ate peaches.

"These are sure good." He wiped the juice as it ran down his beard. "They are so juicy; it's hard to eat them without making a mess." He finished eating a peach and wiped his hands on a napkin.

Carla laughed, "I call them bathtub peaches because they're so juicy they should be eaten over a bathtub."

She wiped her chin with a napkin then took another one and reached across the table to daub Jason's beard.

He caught her hand and kissed her fingers. "That would be a good idea, but I kind of like eating them outside here with you." He winked.

She sat back and they finished wiping peach juice from their faces and hands.

He motioned to the porch swing. "Would you like to move over there and have some more wine?"

She walked over and sat down. He handed her the refilled glass and sat beside her. He removed his cap, set it next to him and ran his hand through his hair. Neither one spoke for a while.

Carla broke the silence. "That's a unique design on your gazebo. Do you spend much time in it?"

"Not much lately. I designed and built it myself."

"Really? I'm impressed. When did you find the time to do that?" She sipped her wine.

"I finished it a few years back. Worked on it on weekends and sometimes after work when I wasn't too tired. There wasn't any need to hurry. It gave me something to do in my spare time, helped take my mind off my personal problems." He looked away for a moment; a brief expression of sadness clouded his face. He turned back and gazed in her eyes. His smile returned. "A friend helped me install the hot tub. Sometimes, I have aches and pains and it's nice to soak in the tub." He rubbed the back of his neck. "It seems to help."

She stood up, walked over to the gazebo and looked inside. Two white wicker chairs and a small glass-covered matching table stood near the large covered tub. She ran her fingers along a smooth-sanded cedar post. She returned to sit beside him.

"You certainly are a skilled woodworker. Where did you learn?"

"From my dad. He was a carpenter. I used to work with him on summer vacations, sometimes on weekends or after school. He was a good teacher, but he can't do much now. Arthritis in his hands and knees is very bad; the results of a lot of years of hard work."

"You must have been a very good student." She raised her eyebrows and smiled.

"I did my best working with wood. Can't say the same about schoolwork. I wasn't a good student, hated doing homework and didn't always pay attention in class. I wasn't at the bottom of my class, but I wasn't destined for a college education." He pushed his toes against the ground and pressed his legs back to rock the chair slightly. "How about you? You never say anything about your job. Do you like accounting?"

She leaned back, relaxed into the cushion. "I was always good at math. It seemed like a good career choice. I suppose it is; supports my horses, but it can boring sometimes." She sighed. "There's so much paperwork and the work-load at tax-time is overwhelming."

He sipped his wine. "I love my job, being out in the woods every day, no paperwork, hardly any stress. Hot or cold weather, and especially rain can make it uncomfortable at times, but I'd rather be outside any day than stuck in an office."

Jason set down his glass and reached for her hand. He caressed her slender fingers, lifted them to his face and slid them gently across his lips. He moved his hands to her head and ran his fingers through the glossy golden brown tresses and gave her feathery light kisses along her earlobes.

"You're so beautiful," he whispered, as he gazed into her heavily-lashed eyes.

"Thank you for saying that, but I think you're biased." Her lips curved into a smile.

"No, I'm not, you are beautiful inside and out. I don't understand how anyone could treat you badly. You just haven't had the right man love you."

"Don't I know it."

"I don't want to push you. I want you to feel comfortable and not like I'm making you do anything you don't want to do. I'm not in a hurry."

She nodded. "I appreciate that."

He wrapped his arms around her and pulled her close. His lips found hers and he kissed her softly. She didn't pull away, so he became bolder. His tongue slipped inside her mouth. The pleasant taste of peach made the kiss all the sweeter.

Carla had anticipated his advance and decided not to spurn him this time. She relaxed and felt herself responding to the warm sensuous feelings. Her body, unused to male attention for such a long time, warmed to his ministrations. Heat surged through her from deep within. Her arms tightened around him and her hands felt the tight muscles of his shoulders and back.

He stopped kissing her mouth and turned his attention to her neck. He unbuttoned the top few buttons of her shirt. Delicate kisses floated down her neck and throat. Gentle fingers stroked her hair. His lips proceeded downward to concentrate on the smooth skin of a full breast. His fingers brushed across the responding hardened nipple; he wanted to be sure she was feeling nothing but pleasure.

A moan formed deep within her throat. Her body arched up towards him, encouraging him. His body reacted to her with a familiar firmness.

He knew he would be unfulfilled, but had already prepared himself for that. He wanted her to trust him and to want him as much as he desired her. Pushing her too far this soon in their relationship might push her away forever. He had to accept his own frustration to allow her the time she needed to accept him. He could do that. Had to do it, for her.

Mustering all his self-control, he rose up and sat back. "We better stop. I want to make sure you are certain of your feelings before we do anything more. I want you to be the one to let me know when you're ready. I know it's still too soon."

"Thank you. I appreciate that." Carla was relieved, but in some ways disappointed. Her body was hot and tingly—craving more. He had sparked a well of wanting. Her quickened heartbeat began to slow as her breath returned to normal rate.

"I didn't do anything to make you uncomfortable, did I?"

"No, it felt really nice. I didn't mind at all." In fact she had enjoyed it. He was so gentle and attentive. It was not something she was used to. Part of her was sorry he stopped, but he was right. It was too soon.

He stood up and walked with discomfort back to the table. "I guess I better get this stuff put away." They carried everything into the house and he loaded the dishwasher.

Carla picked up her bowl. "I'll rinse this out and wash it at home."

"Guess I better get you on the road." They didn't say much as he drove her home. Garth was there to meet her with wagging tail and welcoming tongue.

"I'm happy to see you, too." She rubbed the familiar head. Then he was off to greet Jason.

"How are you, boy?" The dog pressed against Jason, obvious in his desire for another ear rub. He was awarded this pleasure and he moaned in contentment as gentle hands worked the flesh at the base of his ears.

Carla watched his hands working the dog. Garth's pleasure was clear. Part of her regretted they had stopped so soon.

Jason pushed the furry head aside. "That's enough; you'll have to wait till next time, buddy. I have to go."

"Thank you for dinner. I had a wonderful time."

"Can we do it again soon?" He smiled as his fingers lightly brushed across her hand.

"That would be nice."

He gave her one last long kiss. "I'll call you."

She watched as he drove down the driveway and headed out. She patted the top of the dog's head. "Well, what do you think, Garth? He does seem nice, doesn't he?"

Intelligent eyes looked up at her. She knew he couldn't understand, but he was her sounding board most of the time and it was comforting to have him there, her loyal companion. They turned to the house and he followed her inside.

"Oh Garth, what am I going to do? Am I setting myself up to be hurt again?" She flopped down on the couch.

The pink tongue came out and licked her hand. She took the loyal head between her hands and stroked the dense hair.

The phone rang. She picked it up and looked at the caller ID. "Hi Mom."

"How was your dinner date?"

Carla paused. "Oh—it was very nice."

"So you had a good time?"

The word was spoken slowly, drawn out. "Yes."

"You sound uncertain. What's wrong?"

"Oh, you know. He seems too nice. I can't trust my emotions. You know the mistakes I've made."

"Honey, don't judge every man by the few rotten apples you managed to find. Look how blessed I was to have your father."

"Believe me Mom; I know how lucky you were. Dad was super, the best man I know. I don't think there's another man like him."

"Oh, he wasn't quite perfect, he had a few faults, but I miss him every day."

"You had a long happy marriage, thirty-nine years."

"Yes that's true dear, but I'm not dead yet." Her mother paused and then chuckled. "I've got my eye on a man at bridge club."

Carla gasped, "Mom."

"Oh, don't sound surprised. Your dad wouldn't want me to be alone."

"I . . . never really thought about that."

"I'm only sixty-one dear. Plenty of time left." Her mother laughed. "I don't understand why *you're* so determined to torture yourself."

"I'm not miserable. I'm quite happy actually."

"If you say so, but don't be so distrustful. Take a chance."

"I'll think about it."

"You do that. I'm going to bed now."

"Good night, Mom."

"Sweet dreams dear."

In bed, her eyes were closed, but sleep evaded her for hours. She felt Jason's gentle hands on her skin and the pleasure of his warm kisses. *I would have given in.* Her weakness scared her and she panicked. The internal emotional battle remained unresolved and her self-made wall slipped back into place.

Jason whistled all the way home. He cleaned up the dishes and threw a load of clothes into the washing machine. It was 10:30. Normally, he'd be asleep before now, but he didn't feel the least bit tired. For the first time in ages he felt really happy. When he finally went to bed, he closed his eyes and tasted her on his tongue.

\* \* \*

Jason got out of his truck. The hood of his raincoat offered little protection against the weather as the wind blew rain against his face. This was one of those times when his job was less than pleasurable.

Water ran down the middle of the dirt road, creating a furrow that would get wider and deeper in no time unless something was done to alter the course of the flow. He took a shovel out of the truck bed and went to work digging a ditch to divert the rivulet, then stood back and watched with a feeling of satisfaction as the water was redirected rather than eroding the road. Mission accomplished, he tossed the shovel in back and headed to another trouble-spot.

At the end of the day, he stripped out of his wet clothes and took a hot shower. He opened a can and ate a bowl of soup for dinner, then he called Carla. The familiar voice of her answering machine droned in his ear.

"At the sound of the beep, please record your message."

"Carla, it's Jason. Please call me when you get a chance." He sighed and pushed the off button.

*Oh, crap. Where are you? This is the third message I've left. Why aren't you returning my calls?* It was frustrating. After all the progress he'd thought he made with her, why was she doing this now? He couldn't understand. He turned on the TV and watched a couple of sitcoms before going to bed.

Carla listened to the voice message and then erased it. She didn't know what to say to him. She knew she was being unfair after what she had said at the Chinese restaurant about giving him a chance. He deserved a reply.

They'd had a wonderful evening. He was a good cook. She was sure he knew how to please a woman and he'd been so nice to her, but she was doing fine without a man. She was happy. Why take a chance and throw a monkey wrench into her life? She had decided against taking the risk. She knew she should tell him, but she just couldn't face him yet.

## Chapter 23

Opening remarks were finished and the first witness, Detective James Renfield, was sworn in. He was confident and self-controlled. Kitsap County prosecutor Jennifer Lawrence stood before him. The courtroom was filled. The twelve members of the jury, eight woman and four men, focused on the witness.

He was asked to describe the details of the investigation. His testimony was methodical and precise. He took meticulous notes throughout the investigation and the facts were indelibly imprinted in his memory. He had gone over them so many times, nothing was left out. Step by step, he laid out the case.

Photographs of the victims and their car, the Collier search site and the murder scene provided the jury with graphic detail of the horrific nature of the crime and the ruthlessness of the defendant. The gun, bloody clothing, shoes, license plates, mushroom collection bag, plastic bag with blood of both victims and zip ties were and all items belonging to the victims were into evidence.

The attorney for the defense, Tyson, rose and objected to the gun being included. "Your Honor, there's no evidentiary link between that weapon and my client."

The DA countered, "Your Honor, the prosecution will prove beyond a shadow of a doubt that this gun was indeed used by the defendant to execute the victims."

"Overruled."

The prosecution continued to question Detective Renfield. DNA results had come back, irrefutable evidence tying the victims to the suspect. Greg Collier sat throughout the testimony, unemotional; his steely eyes glared straight ahead.

The victims' tearful family members heard once again the grim circumstances that ended the lives of their loved ones. Members of the jury listened intently as Renfield laid out the case. His first day of testimony ended and court adjourned, to reconvene in the morning.

Three days into the trial, the prosecutor finished her interrogation of the witness and it was time for cross-examination. Dale Tyson approached the witness stand. He confronted Renfield and tried to punch holes in the prosecution's case by insinuating the police had framed his client. That tactic didn't hold water and it was a feeble attempt to discredit the detectives' labors. Renfield held up well and his testimony was unassailable. He stepped down off the witness stand, satisfied the jury would recognize the truth.

Following the defense attorney's cross-examination, the judge asked the DA if she had any more questions for the witness.

Jennifer Lawrence stood and faced the judge. "No Your Honor, but we reserve the right to call him at a later date. I would like to call Roger Dirndle of the Kitsap County Crime Lab to the stand.

The forensic expert explained the blood spatter on clothing and shoes, striation on the bullets matching the gun and he correlated the DNA match of the victims' blood on the plastic bag found where the car was parked as well as on items of clothing that were tied to Greg Collier. Shoes matching plaster casts taken at the pond site and confirmed to be Collier's were presented. He explained the process of making plaster casts of the footprints and matching them to the soles of the shoes, and demonstrated how wear marks on the inside of the shoes corresponded to the suspect's feet. Tire treads from the suspect's

Chevy Blazer were an identical match to tread marks found at the crime scene.

After two more days of testimony by Roger Dirndle it was time for the prosecution to question the witness. Tyson made little progress in refuting the evidence and the defense spent only a few hours on cross-exam.

Compelling evidence mounted against the defendant, but it was still circumstantial. They were a week and a half into the trial and had yet to hear from other witnesses.

Jason Gerard was subpoenaed to testify. He took his seat before the court. Hatless, hair neatly combed, beard trimmed and wearing a navy blue blazer, matching slacks and a pale blue shirt that he'd been told accentuated his clear blue eyes, he completed the ensemble with a patriotic red, white and blue tie. He was proud to display his love of country. He seldom dressed up, but he wanted to represent the prosecution with pride and dignity.

Jennifer Lawrence started questioning. "Please state your name."

"Jason Gerard."

"Now, please tell the court how you discovered the bodies of Tim Sutton and Janice Williams."

Jason sometimes glanced toward the jury as he repeated the sequence of events the day he found the car containing the bodies at the bottom of the pond on the tree farm. His matter-of-fact composure broke down as once again he had to relive the horrific condition of the victims. The smell of decay—of rotting bodies—the assault on his senses returned. Several members of the jury dabbed tears in their own eyes as Jason choked up and struggled to formulate his words. It was a difficult day.

He testified about the investigators' conduct and integrity during the investigation, and described the point of entry used by the perpetrators to gain access onto the property. He looked Collier directly in the eye. It gave him some degree of satisfaction to know that he was in some way personally responsible for removing this evil criminal from society.

Cross-examination by Dale Tyson was not too intense. Jason's testimony, while important, was not a particular target for the defense. He was only on the witness stand for a few hours. It was over without his integrity being called into question. Never-the-less, he was relieved when questioning was over and he was asked to step down. Court adjourned for the day.

Jason walked out of the courtroom, paused to get a drink at the water fountain. Renfield saw him and waited.

"You did well today," Renfield said. "I know it wasn't easy."

"No . . . it wasn't." He brushed a hand across his lips. "I want to be there when the verdict comes in. Can you call and let me know?"

"Of course, I'd be happy to."

"I appreciate that."

Jason left the courthouse and started home, his emotions in turmoil. The ages of the victims had been similar to those of his children. He couldn't help but feel compassion and sorrow for the victims' families.

The sight and smell of the corpses brought back memories of another time of death. Being a war vet, he wanted to put the horror of some of his own experiences behind him. Sometimes, nightmares of his buddies and civilians being blown apart by roadside bombs still haunted him—especially the children. Finding the bodies of Tim Sutton and Janice Williams revived those old memories and feelings.

He hadn't talked about it to anyone, but he was struggling with those demons again. He never wanted to relive those traumatic events. It had taken him so long to come to terms with what he had seen and done in Iraq and Afghanistan. The anguish of taking a life, even when it meant saving your own and the lives of your comrades was hard to live with. He still saw the faces. The victims of a roadside bomb attack. A buddy killed; his arm and head blown off. Another, survived, but lost a leg. When it all came flooding back, he tried his best to put it behind him and move on with his life. It was so hard.

Now, here it was again, coming back to haunt him. Like a rerun of an old movie—it played over and over. He wished he could rewrite his history, erase the memories forever and replace them with more pleasant scenes. He ran to his truck and headed home through a driving rain.

At first the rain had felt cleansing, soothing, nourishing, but now it was an adversary pounding down from the skies: incessant flooding, eroding, washing away people's homes. It became a killer: toppling trees, forcing wild animals and people from their shelters, victims seeking refuge from the unrelenting weather. It made his job miserable. He ended up wet and cold no matter what he did. Roads washed out. He spent his days digging trenches and checking on vulnerable locations, vigilant efforts to prevent disaster and keep problems to a minimum. It was exhausting and depressing.

The rain dampened his spirits as well as the ground. It wasn't just the rain. On top of everything else, he hadn't heard from Carla in weeks. Forging a relationship with her had been an uphill battle, but at least for a while, everything seemed to be going fine as far as he could tell. She obviously enjoyed his company, he seemed to be gaining ground, but then without explanation she avoided him. The miserable weather was a fitting backdrop for his mood.

He longed for those warm, sunny, glorious days of summer: days full of fun and companionship, riding free on the back of his horse, scents of fir and flowers in the air and the wonderful woman on horseback, riding nearby, German shepherd at her side. They had so much in common and seemed so comfortable together. How could she deny that?

Her sexuality taunted him: the feel of her soft fragrant skin, luxurious glossy hair, the narrow valley between her warm full breasts, and inviting sensual lips. He wanted her, craved her, with every part of his being, but it wasn't to be. He was unable to conquer those demons from her past: those other men whose reach and power far exceeded his own.

He imagined he could feel her soft skin and warm passionate kisses. His blood flow surged and his body heated up at the mere thought of her. She overwhelmed his thoughts and ravaged his soul. Everywhere he went; everything he did. There she was: plaguing him, plying him, torturing him, never far from his thoughts, beautiful, alluring, bright—unattainable.

Instead of going straight home, an irresistible force drew him to the tree farm. The windshield wipers worked overtime as he stared out the window.

Rain hammered melodically on the metal hood and roof of his pickup. Pregnant drops poured from the angry sky, pelting the water and sending countless splashing ripplets into the murky gray pond.

Memories of the two murder victims came flooding back. He visualized them, hidden beneath the surface in their watery grave, lost to their families forever. He grieved—not just for the man and woman he hardly knew—but for Carla, lost to him beneath the surface of a deep, impenetrable wall of fear. Fear that resided beneath the soft skin and firm muscles of the strong, self-confident, capable woman who allowed bad memories to overshadow the present, denying her the love and happiness that should be hers—and his.

Tears welled in his eyes; overcome by wrenching sadness and grief. He suddenly felt threatened, doomed by all the negative thoughts and vibrations clutching at his world. He had to put it all behind him. Put *her* behind him.

Jason conceded defeat. He pounded the steering wheel with his fist. *I'm done with her, done trying to get past her emotional baggage, done with her mind games.* He was resigned to letting her go and live alone. He'd throw himself into his work. He'd done it before. He could do it again. He wiped his sleeve across his liquid eyes, put the truck in reverse, turned it around and headed home.

Back at the house, he trudged through the rivulets and puddles to feed his grumbling horses. Dampness permeated everything. It was hard to keep down mold and mildew. He mucked out the stalls and tossed down fresh shavings and straw. He knew the bedding would end up wet soon, but he tried to keep the horses as comfortable as possible. They chewed grain as he stuffed hay into the racks.

The cats meowed and rubbed against his legs, purring as he reached down to pet them. He changed the litter box and filled their dishes with food and water. They refused to go outside in this weather, and he could hardly blame them. It was really nasty out there.

He finished up and went back to the house, stripped out of his boots, rain gear and wet clothing and took a long hot shower. After drying off, he pulled on jeans and a sweatshirt settled down on the sofa in front of the TV with his usual bowl of cereal for dinner.

The phone rang. He looked at the caller ID, Northwest Tree Farm. "Hello."

"Jason."

"What's up Ray?"

"Kitsap County's got a washout on Harmon Road. I've given permission for the county to have access to land on the backside. I need you to meet with the Sherriff's Department at the washout. You'll have to plan the route and work out the details with the Department of Transportation. Sorry to send you out late in this weather, but they're relying on us."

"I'll leave right away."

"Thanks."

Jason closed the phone. "Dammit!" He held the bowl to his lips and sucked down the rest of dinner, then carried the dish to the sink.

Jason pulled on a dry set of rain gear and boots and went out again. The wipers slapped across the windshield unable to keep up with the curtain of rain. He drove slowly, barely able to see the center line, turned off the highway and crossed the county line. He turned off the arterial and pulled over behind a Kitsap County Sherriff's car. A KOMO news crew was already on site. A group of people were gathered at the end of a line of vehicles. Barricades blocked the road. A deputy stood behind the blockade. He waved Jason around.

Jason spotted Deputy Stevens at the far end of the crowd. He sloshed through a foot of mud, debris and water. The sound of roaring water drowned out the drumming rain. He worked his way between the bystanders to where Stevens stood.

Jason was aghast. "Holy crap!"

A river raged where a shallow stream once flowed through a huge culvert beneath the asphalt road. The pavement was gone, torn away along with trees and bushes. The great ragged gash in the landscape washed out the entire road for a width of twenty feet. Onlookers gaped at the result of the water's power.

The deputy signaled. Jason maneuvered to Steven's side.

Steven's said, "What do you think. Really something isn't it?"

Jason nodded toward the far side of the road. "Glad I don't live up there."

"Me too, those folks are all stranded, unable to leave or return home. Looks like it's going to be that way for a while. There's no quick fix. That's why I called. Glad Ray's willing to allow the locals to drive across Northwest Tree Farm land until the road can be repaired. We need that route ASAP." Stevens tilted his plastic covered hat. Water poured off the brim and splashed onto his yellow rubber pant leg.

Jason looked around at the glum faces of soaked bystanders. A number of them were people he knew or at least recognized. They were all waiting for him to solve their problem, to open the tree farm and let them drive home. A loud breath escaped between his pursed lips as he mulled over the logistics of Steven's request. "It's do-able. Not sure how long it'll take me to get things set up."

Steven's said, "Sorry to hit you with this, but there really isn't any other solution, no alternate route."

"I know. This has never happened here before. Most other washouts have detours. They may be long and a hell of an inconvenience, but at least people aren't trapped." Jason wiped water out of his eyes. "I'll get this worked out."

A clerk he'd known for years who worked at the local grocery store in Key Center, Diane Wellers, walked up to him. "Jason, they're telling us we'll be able to drive through Northwest Tree Farm land. Is that true?"

"Well, that's the plan; just heard about it myself. It's going to take me some time to work it out. Not sure how long it's going to take. I'm going to have to get busy working on it. Don't know if I can get it done tonight, but I'll do my best to get it open as soon as I can."

"I hope so." Her voice was strained. "My kids are home alone."

The KOMO news team moved closer. The reporter stood beside them, held up the microphone. "Deputy Stevens, what can you tell us about the problem here? How are people going to get to their homes? What about the disabled people? Will emergency vehicles be able to get through?"

Stevens said, "It's a tough situation every way you look at it. Right now, there is no way back there, but we're in the process of working things out with Northwest Tree Farm." He placed a hand on Jason's shoulder. "This is a representative from the tree farm. He'll be the one working out the transportation route. He can answer some of your questions."

The reporter shifted to Jason. He answered the questions as well as he could. "I'll know more once I get things mapped out. I need to leave and get busy if I'm going to get done tonight."

He turned away, passed Stevens on the way out. "Tom, I'll call you soon as I have a route ready."

"I'll be here until I get your call."

Jason shook himself off before he got in the truck. He headed toward home, pulled in at the tree farm section he needed to open, and unlocked the gate, closed it behind him and headed east. Rivulets of water flowed down the dirt road eroding it into a ragged streambed. *I'll have to fix that.* The tires spun in deep mud. The road took a turn heading north. At a fork he headed right, east. He came to the gate at the other end.

At least most of the road was good. He'd have post signs and check on the county road at this end. He unlocked the gate and drove onto the gravel road. Not too bad. He checked his cellphone. No bars.

Jason headed back and stopped where the road was washing away. He got out, took a shovel from the back, worked on the ditch at the side of the road and managed to divert the flow off the road and into the ditch. That would take care of it for a while.

He drove to where he knew he had a signal and called Deputy Stevens. "Got a plan worked out. I need some detour signs and direction arrows. After we get the signs in place, I'll open up the gates. We've got to limit it to local traffic. These roads weren't meant to handle a lot of cars, no rock, just dirt and they're pretty muddy."

Stevens said, "I'll let you know when I can get someone from the DOT out there. There overstretched now."

"I can be out in fifteen minutes."

"Thanks."

"I'll be waiting for your call." Jason closed the phone and put it back in his pocket.

Jason met Deputy Stevens and the DOT workers at 8:30 p.m. They stopped where necessary to post signs. The KOMO news team was at the site again to publicize the altered traffic route.

## Chapter 24

Friday morning, court resumed. Michael Freeman was seated on the witness stand. He wore a gray suit and tie. His shorn blond hair was combed and his blue eyes were bright—drug-free.

Jennifer Lawrence stepped up to the witness stand. "Do you recognize the defendant?"

Collier fixed a cold stare on the witness. Several members of the jury reacted to the menacing look in those cold gray eyes.

Freeman glanced at Collier then turned away, not wanting to look his former cohort in the eye. "Yeah, that's Greg Collier."

"What is your relationship to the defendant?"

"We was friends. I helped him out at his place."

"What sort of things did you do?"

"Growin' pot, takin' cars apart, cookin' meth, some other stuff." Freeman raised his hand to his mouth and gnawed on a fingernail.

"Mr. Freeman, whose cars were you taking apart?"

He continued to chew on the nail, didn't respond to the question.

"Mr. Freeman, I repeat, whose cars were you taking apart?"

He took his finger out of his mouth and looked up. "They was stole."

"So, the defendant was running a chop shop at his home?" The prosecutor turned to look at the jury.

"Yeah." Freeman rubbed his knuckles against his thighs.

She sauntered back to her desk, turned and looked into the faces of the jurors, walked back toward the witness and stopped in front of him. "Collier had a large marijuana growing business and he was operating a meth lab?"

"Yeah." He looked away and focused on the floor.

"Did he have lots of visitors?"

"Just people buyin' drugs, no one we didn't know. Greg didn't like strangers droppin' by."

"Do you remember where you were on March 18th of last year, Mr. Freeman?"

"Yeah, I was out at Greg's place."

Tyson was on his feet. "Objection. The witness can't possibly remember what date it was."

Lawrence looked at Freeman. "How were you sure of the date?"

Freeman looked her in the eye. "Oh, I remember all right. Ain't never gonna forget that day. Wish I could. That's my brother's birthday. Same day Greg shot those people."

"Overruled."

Tyson sat down.

Lawrence continued. "Where were you when you first saw the victims, Timothy Sutton and Janice Williams?"

"I went out back to work in the weed patch."

"You are referring to the field of marijuana you were all growing out behind the house at the Collier farm?"

"Yeah." He glanced up briefly.

She walked over to her desk and picked up some pictures. "Your honor, I am entering these photographs of the marijuana patch into evidence." She held up the photos and showed them to the jury.

She stood before the witness and continued questioning. "Would you please tell the court what you saw and heard?"

"I heard voices out behind the weed. I couldn't hear what they was sayin', so I went back and got Greg."

"What was Greg's reaction when you told him there were people out there?"

"He got real pissed off."

"What did he do?"

"He checked his gun, grabbed gloves, some zip-ties and said 'followed me.'"

Jennifer walked back to the prosecution's desk and returned to the front of the courtroom carrying a plastic bag with cut zip-ties inside. "Are these the ties Greg used?"

"Guess so. Looks like 'em. 'Cept they wasn't cut."

She held the bag for members of the jury to see. "These were cut off the victims' wrists after their bodies were recovered."

The color drained from Freeman's face and he looked back down at the floor.

She entered them into evidence, then picked up another bag of uncut zip-ties and held it up for the jury to see. "These were found at the defendant's house. They are identical to the ones found on the victims."

The prosecution continued with the testimony of Michael Freeman for two days. He described the murder in detail.

Members of the jury focused on him throughout his chilling testimony. Some of them jotted down notes. Occasionally, they glanced at the defendant.

Greg Collier showed no remorse for the crimes he had committed. His demeanor did not earn him any sympathy in the eyes of the jurors.

Jennifer Lawrence was in the final stages of the prosecution's testimony. She wanted to make sure Collier was proven guilty without any doubt to be the major perpetrator of this crime rather than the man on the witness stand.

"Would you say you feared losing your own life if you didn't do what the defendant ordered you to do?"

"Yeah, Greg was pissed those people showed up. He didn't want 'em goin' to the cops and tellin' 'em what we was doin'."

Freeman looked at the prosecutor and then turned to look at the members of the jury. "If I didn't help him, he woulda killed me for sure."

"You are quite certain of that?"

"Yeah, he can be real mean if he's pissed off. I didn't wanna be dead meat."

"How did you feel after the murders?"

Freeman licked dry lips, and swallowed, "It made me sick. My gut was killin' me for days. I couldn't sleep. I kept seein' 'em in my head. That lady cryin' kept comin' back. I still can't sleep thinkin' 'bout it."

"So, you were an unwilling accomplice in the whole affair." She looked at the defendant who glared back.

Freeman's voice was low, barely audible. "Yeah."

"Can you repeat that louder please?"

"Yeah," He reached up and rubbed his eyes. "I helped him . . . but I didn't want to."

"What did Greg do to you after you were arrested?"

"He threatened to kill me if I squealed. He stabbed me in the side in jail. Cut my lung. I coulda died."

She turned to face the jury when she asked the next question. "So it was only after you were almost murdered yourself that you agreed to testify against him?"

"Yeah, the cops promised to keep him away from me. He's a mean son-of-a-bitch. I knew he'd try again."

She faced Freeman again. "Do you still fear for your life if he is not kept away?"

"Yeah, I might not be so lucky next time."

"Objection.

"Sustained," the judge announced, "strike that from the record."

Jennifer Lawrence stepped back and turned to address the judge. "I'm finished with this witness, Your Honor." She walked to the prosecution's desk and took her seat.

It was 3:00 p.m. Friday afternoon. The judge adjourned the court until Monday morning. Everyone rose and filed out.

Jennifer felt confident the defense would not be able to damage their case. Freeman's testimony had been solid. She was going home to relax in a hot bath.

The weekend would provide a bit of a respite from court. She loved her job, but at times it could be stressful and depressing. The viciousness of crimes and the lack of compassion shown by perpetrators could sometimes get her down. She made it her absolute goal to put away as many of them as she could. It was all she could do to try and make the world a safer place, at least her small part of it.

Two hours later, Jennifer lay back in the tub and listened to the familiar cadence of rain hammering on the roof and sliding down the windowpanes. All this rain was getting to be hard to take, days on end. She was glad she didn't have to work outside. She closed her eyes and let the warmth of the water cleanse away the tribulations of the week.

* * *

Carla changed out of her wet clothes and turned on the TV. A reporter stood in front of a crowd of people in the rain.

A woman in a hooded raincoat was speaking into the microphone. "I was the last car to get across before it washed out. I couldn't get home until the next morning."

The voice sounded familiar. Carla squinted, got up and moved closer to the TV, studied the woman's face. Diane, the checker at the market. Washed out where? The camera scanned the crowd.

The reporter said, "It could be weeks before Harmon Road in Kitsap County is repaired after the washout yesterday leaving seventy-five homeowners without access. Northwest Tree Farm has opened their land to allow local residents to drive through."

He moved through the crowd and stopped beside a man. "Here's Jason Gerard, spokesman for Northwest Tree Farm."

Carla's eyes were glued to the screen. She hadn't seen Jason for a couple of months. Now, seeing him on TV she was fixated, couldn't take her eyes off him.

He spoke next. "The unpaved maintenance roads will be open to local residents or emergency use only. They aren't suitable for high volume traffic. Homeowners can use our back roads until the county road is open. We'll be keeping our land available as long as necessary." He stopped talking.

The reporter lowered the mike, moved away, interviewed a deputy, and then a few more people in the crowd. The camera panned the water flowing where the road used to be. The segment ended and switched to a fatality car wreck on I-5 near Tukwila.

Carla didn't move. She sat perfectly still, heart pounding. Her chest felt strangely heavy. *What's wrong with me? Am I having a heart attack?* She closed her eyes and took deep breaths. The feeling dissipated and she felt normal again.

Garth had cocked his head, looked at the TV when he heard Jason's voice. Now, he moved to her side and licked her hand.

Monday morning Public Defender Dale Tyson shook out his umbrella and closed it up as he entered the courthouse. He knew he faced an uphill battle, and if the truth were known, he really didn't give a shit. He had a strong dislike of the defendant. It was his duty to provide adequate defense, but this guy was pure evil. There was no way he would get off and the world would be a better place with him off the street.

He was seated at the defense desk absentmindedly thumbing through a stack of paperwork. He was adjusting his glasses when guards brought in his client.

Collier sat down beside him and asked, "Are you going to call me to testify on my own behalf?"

"I don't think that's a good idea. I'm going to cross-examine Michael Freeman."

There was no way having Collier on the witness stand would aid his case. The 6'4" bulky frame with the permanent scowl was the devil incarnate. He exuded hatred and loathing. The jury would never accept him as a sympathetic character.

The gavel was struck. The judge announced, "Court is now in session."

Tyson stood and said, "I would like to call Michael Freeman to the stand." The defense prepared to cross-examine the witness.

Two officers brought Michael Freeman into the courtroom. The bailiff reminded him he was still under oath after he took his seat on the witness stand.

Tyson stepped from behind his desk and approached Freeman. "So, you were the one who discovered the victims while they were out behind the marijuana?" Tyson wanted to remind the jury.

"Yeah." Freeman looked down at the floor, avoided Collier's venomous eyes.

The PD pointed his finger at Freeman. "It was really you who pulled the gun on the victims and executed them, wasn't it? Now, you're trying to frame my client."

Freeman shrieked. "No way, man! I didn't want 'em dead! I didn't know Greg was gonna kill 'em. I thought he'd just run 'em off. Scare 'em—you know—I ain't no murderer!" Hands shaking, the witness twisted in his seat.

"That's what you'd like this court to believe." Tyson nodded toward the jury.

Freeman's high pitched screech echoed through the courtroom. "That's the truth."

"You're a regular Boy Scout. Isn't it true you got out of the death penalty by testifying against my client?"

Collier sneered cold as a snake at his one-time friend and partner in crime.

"I said I'd testify, but I sure as hell didn't murder 'em. I done a lot o' shit in my life, but I ain't ever killed nobody!" Beads of perspiration formed on his forehead as he fidgeted in his chair.

"That's what you'd like us to believe?" Tyson turned his back on Freeman and paced in front of the jurors.

Jennifer Lawrence stood up. "Objection. The prosecution's badgering the witness."

"Sustained," the judge ruled.

"I withdraw the question." Tyson knew the jury would still have that thought in their minds. He didn't believe it would make any difference anyway. He finished his line of questioning and announced, "The defense rests."

Closing arguments followed: first the defense. The Public Defender watched the jurors as he made his final arguments.

Several jurors shook their heads in disbelief as the defense attorney laid the blame on Freeman. It was obvious they did not believe his client was innocent.

Jennifer Lawrence followed up with the summation for the prosecution. Members of the jury paid close attention as she emphasized the case against the defendant, point by point.

Everyone stepped out of the courtroom into the melee in the hall. Members of the news media awaited the opportunity to get statements from everyone involved. It was a relief to have it all behind them. Jennifer broke free from the media blitz and joined Renfield as he walked down the steps.

"How long do you think it will take the jury to reach a verdict?" Renfield asked. It was more of a rhetorical question; he didn't really expect an answer.

"I don't know. I don't think it will be that long. Sentencing may take longer. This was a capital offense. This case was pretty cut and dried, I'm optimistic it will turn out right."

"It's tough to know what's inside the heads of the jurors. I won't relax until the verdict is in." Renfield reached the door first and held it for her.

Jennifer opened her umbrella as she stepped outside. A gust of wind caught her umbrella and she fought to keep it from turning inside out. Raindrops battered the sidewalk and formed rushing silver rivers that flowed into deep rippling puddles in the street.

"You think we'll see the end of this rain anytime soon?" She was tired of fighting the weather.

"I don't know. It's duck weather for sure. I may just have to grow webbed feet if this keeps up." He grinned, but the monotonous rainy days bleeding into one another sucked energy from the saturated earth and its drenched inhabitants. He hoped it would let up soon.

"Give me a call when the jury comes in. I don't want to miss that," he called out as he ran toward his car.

"Sure thing, I expect it will be some time tomorrow." She clutched her coat tighter around her until she reached her car.

"I'll be waiting to hear from you."

He slid inside watching water drip onto his seat. The car splashed through a puddle out of the parking lot, sending a large spray as it entered the heavy flow coming down the street.

\* \* \*

The call came in at two p.m. The jury had reached a verdict. Jim Renfield phoned Jason to let him know.

Jason decided to drive along the waterfront rather than take the more direct route into town. Looking out across Sinclair Inlet, he could barely make out the aircraft carriers and other ships moored at Puget Sound Naval Shipyard in Bremerton. They were almost hidden from view by the veil of rain that drilled down without letup.

He was intent on the road ahead, listening to the thwop thwop thwop of the windshield wipers as they worked to keep up with the constant flow of rain battering the window. A deafening rumble erupted from the hillside above on the right. Saturated earth on the cliff next to the road broke away. Trees, brush, rocks, and mud tore free and tumbled in a nightmarish cascade down the vertical slope. Tons of muck and vegetation careened at breakneck speed in a devouring mass, wiping out everything in their path.

The landslide slammed into Jason's truck. The passenger side and front end bore the full brunt of the force, collapsing into the driver's side. Glass shattered and bending steel screeched as the impact flipped the truck on its side and pushed it across the highway, encasing Jason between layers of torn metal, mud and debris. He had no time to react—the thunderous crash and pain—then everything went black.

\* \* \*

The courtroom was filled, everyone awaiting the outcome. The jury foreman handed the paper to the bailiff who took it to the judge.

After reading the results, the judge turned to the jury. "How do you find the defendant on the first charge of murder in the first degree?"

The foreman looked straight at the defendant, said. "Guilty."

"How do you find the defendant on the second charge of murder in the first degree?"

"Guilty."

A collective sigh and subdued cheer rang through the courtroom as the verdict was read. Family members and friends of the victims exchanged hugs and expressed relief. Nothing could bring their loved ones back, but at least the deaths would not go unpunished.

"Court is adjourned." The crowd made their way to the hall.

Renfield smiled broadly. "Thank God that's over. Job well done, madam prosecutor."

"Thank you for the compliment, but without solid police work and that confession, it would have been a tough one. Thank you for making my job a lot easier. Now I can go home and relax."

He held the door as she stepped outside and opened her umbrella. He followed.

"Have a good evening." She stepped lightly trying to avoid puddles.

"You, too." He ran for the car.

## Chapter 25

Carla trudged across the yard, splashing through puddles and the deepening stream that eroded her driveway. As she entered the house, a sheet of water blasted inside before she could close the door behind her. She slipped out of her raincoat, pulled off her boots and peeled off her soaking wet jeans. Water pooled on the floor beneath her dripping clothes. Her animals were fed, the stalls cleaned, and she was wet and miserable. Even Garth hadn't wanted to go outside; he welcomed her back, licking her cold wet hand with his long pink tongue. Rain hammered the roof and windows and poured out of the downspouts, blasting a tympanic cacophony as the surging weather assaulted everything in its path. *When will the rain end?*

She put on a pair of sweats, hung up her sopping clothes in the laundry room, set her boots on a stand to dry, and mopped up the floor. She ladled some clam chowder from a pot on the stove before sitting in front of the TV with her hot bowl of soup. Picking up the remote, she switched channels to watch the local news. The verdict was in for the Greg Collier trial: Guilty.

*Thank goodness.* She spooned a mouthful of chowder, swirled it on her tongue, swallowed. "Mmmmm. This is perfect for a rainy day," she told her dog.

The news focus changed to the weather: flooding and power outages, more mud slides throughout the area; another land slide blocking Highway 166 in Port Orchard; the road was closed indefinitely. The news anchor talked about a single victim who had been airlifted to Harborview Hospital, condition unknown. As the camera panned across the slide, a red pickup truck was visible, crushed beneath a mass of mud and debris. The identity of the victim would not be released until the family could be notified.

The color drained from Carla's face as she recognized the familiar red truck. She couldn't be certain; most of it was buried. It couldn't be Jason. Maybe it was another old red Chevy. Her hands began to tremble and all the breath seemed to leave her body. A sudden chill left her goose-fleshed skin shivering out of control. Her stomach was doing summersaults. She pushed away the remains of her soup and rushed into the bathroom. Her legs felt weak, wobbly. She pressed a hand against the wall to keep from losing her balance. Her head hung over the toilet bowl. What food she'd already consumed landed in the water before swirling down the drain. A glass of water failed to rinse the sour taste from her mouth.

She rose and tilted her head back forcing air into her lungs in long, rapid deep breaths. Unfamiliar sensations vibrated throughout her body. *When did I see him last? On TV, last week. Before that—months ago—August.*

She had avoided him, unable to reconcile her conflicted emotions. Sudden terror overcame her. *Is he in the hospital? How is he? Maybe it's not him.* She struggled to convince herself. Tears rolled down her cheeks. *I have to know.*

She got out his business card and punched in the numbers for his home phone. The voice she heard was a recording. Next she tried his cell phone, another recording. The phone company's message: "The number you dialed is unavailable at this time."

Her heart hammered against the walls of her chest. Queasy and out of breath, she gasped for air. Her hands shook as she called information to get the number for Harborview Hospital in Seattle. If he had been taken there, the main trauma center for the whole area, his condition had to be very serious; otherwise, he would have been taken to Harrison Hospital in Bremerton. Her trembling fingers misdialed the number. She pushed the off button and tried again.

A receptionist answered the phone and Carla struggled to get the words out. "Has Jason Gerard been admitted?"

"I'm sorry. I can't give out information on patients due to the patient privacy act," the voice on the other end of the line replied.

"But I think I know the victim. I'm a friend."

"I'm sorry. I'm not allowed to give you any information."

"Damn!" She slammed down the phone and hurried to her bedroom.

Garth looked at her, head tilting downward, from side to side, in canine fashion.

She threw off her clothes, pulled on a sweatshirt, pair of jeans, and shoes, grabbed a raincoat, umbrella and her purse and rushed out the door. Oh my God—the stove. She fought the key in the lock, whisked the pot off the burner, turned off the gas and put the leftover chowder into the fridge. Gravel flew from behind her wheels as she peeled out of the driveway.

"I'll check his house. Maybe he was just out in the barn." She hardly recognized her own cracking voice.

She pulled up at his house. No one was home. The truck wasn't there. She ran out to the barn.

All three cats meowed in unison. She filled up their dish, found a box, poured in more food. The grumbling horses were given extra grain and she threw a whole bale of hay into each stall. Carla wasn't sure how long it would be before someone would be back. At least this would keep them fed for a couple of days. They had plenty of water. The rain took care of that.

Her fingers drummed with impatience on the steering wheel as she waited for the next ferry. Time lapsed at a glacial pace. The blast of the horn announced the arrival of the Issaquah. A worker lowered the ramp on the dock and pedestrians rushed off, followed by a steady stream of vehicles. Finally, it was time for her to drive on and a crewman directed her to a lane. She turned off the engine and set the emergency brake.

She decided to get out of her car and go up to the passenger deck to have a cup of coffee for the duration of the trip. She picked up a magazine and sat by the window. She thumbed through the pages, but her eyes only saw Jason.

A voice boomed over the intercom. "Arriving at Vashon Island."

They pulled up to the dock. Carla was almost unaware of the thumping and rumbling of cars as they rolled across the metal deck and up the ramp. Another blast of the horn and they were underway.

Puget Sound was choppy; foam-laced white caps danced on the steel gray waves. Rain cascaded against the windows in silver sheets as it machine-gunned the swaying craft. The dock was coming up fast.

Carla was already in her car strapping on her seat belt as the horn blasted.

The voice announced over the loudspeaker. "Arriving at Fauntleroy. Return to your vehicles."

Thirty-five minutes later she pulled into the hospital parking lot. She rushed inside and inquired at the desk, "Can you please tell me where to find Jason Gerard?"

The receptionist looked up. "Are you a family member?"

"No. I'm a friend."

"I'm sorry. I can't give out any information unless you're a family member."

"Ohhhhh . . . I just drove all the way from Port Orchard. Can't you even give me his room number? He'd want to see me."

"Only his family members will be allowed to see him."

"Oh, God," Carla sobbed. Her knees buckled. She grabbed the edge of the countertop to support herself.

"Let me page his family. Maybe they can help you," the receptionist offered.

"Thank you." Carla hadn't ever met anyone from Jason's family and didn't know if he'd even told them about her. If he had, they might not want anything to do with her. She certainly hadn't behaved in a manner that deserved their kindness.

"You can wait in the lobby." The receptionist pointed to a seated area.

Carla had no idea what to do. She clutched a paper cup of coffee that had long since grown cold. Her shoes squeaked as she paced back and forth across the well-worn vinyl floor.

A young woman appeared at the reception desk, "You paged me?"

"You're a member of Jason Gerard's family?"

"Yes, he's my father."

"There's a woman here who wants to see him. We aren't allowed to give out information to anyone other than family members. I told her she could speak to one of you. She has brown shoulder-length hair and she's wearing jeans and a navy-blue sweatshirt. You'll find her in the lobby."

Carla watched a young woman approach. Something about her was vaguely familiar: her clear blue eyes and the full shape of her lips. The woman's eyelids were red and puffy from crying; her lips were drawn and taut. She raked a hand through her short-bobbed brown hair.

Her voice broke as she spoke, "Excuse me, you were asking about Jason Gerard?"

"Yes, I'm a friend . . . Carla Summers . . . I saw his truck on the news . . . I had to come."

"I'm sure Dad would appreciate that." Tears rolled down her high rounded cheeks. "I'm his daughter, Becky. Dad told us about you."

"He did?" Carla hadn't expected that. "How is he? Has he said anything?"

"We don't know yet. He's still in surgery. He's been unconscious since they brought him in." She paused to pull a tissue out of her purse and blow her nose before continuing. "Dad has some broken bones: a leg, an arm, a few ribs and a head injury, but we won't know how serious it is until he wakes up." Tears welled in her eyes.

Carla reached out and took Becky's hand. "Ohhhhh." Strength rushed out of her. Her knees felt weak and she felt as though she might collapse in a heap on the floor.

A young man walked up. "What's up, Sis?" His voice sounded much like Jason's. His eyes were a deeper shade of blue, but the nose and lips were the same. He didn't have a beard; instead, a narrow mustache lined his upper lip. He had a full head of brown hair.

Becky touched her brother's shoulder. "This is Dad's friend, Carla."

He reached out his hand. "I'm Jeff, nice to meet you."

He noticed her trembling and took her arm to help steady her. "We were going to the cafeteria. Why don't you come along and join us?"

"Yes, I'd like that." The slightest hint of a smile crossed her lips.

They sat down with their trays. Carla sipped her coffee, but she couldn't bring herself to pick at the salad on her plate. It was the only thing that had looked even remotely appealing. She had no appetite.

"Dad told us he was seeing someone, but he didn't tell us much about you." Becky set down her coffee and took a bite of a sandwich.

"I'm afraid there wasn't much to say." Carla was ashamed to admit. "I haven't seen him lately."

Jeff looked directly into her eyes as he spoke. "Dad is a really great guy. Mom didn't give him a fair shake. I don't understand why she wanted a divorce. He's a workaholic, so he was gone a lot. He always took good care of us. He worked hard to send both of us to college. He never went himself, so it was important to him."

Becky brushed tears from her cheeks, struggling to maintain her composure as memories flooded back. "He took us camping and fishing every summer, and riding on weekends. We always had horses and we did 4-H. Mom was usually the one who took us to meetings and school events, but Dad went when he could. He supported us so we could do everything we wanted to do."

Listening to them, Carla felt nothing but regret as she sat there. Jason had been kind to her, yet she had stopped returning his calls and had pushed him away. Fear had kept her from accepting the attentions of a very nice man. She prayed he would recover and she would be given another chance to rectify that.

The thought that she might never get the opportunity brought tears to her eyes. They came in an uncontrollable flood and rolled down her cheeks, splashing onto the tabletop.

"I'm sorry." She picked up her napkin and blew her nose. Jeff passed her some more, and she dabbed her eyes and dried her damp cheeks.

The tears weren't just for the predicament Jason was in. They were a reaction to the sudden realization she had turned away from happiness, had denied Jason contentment as well. Not because of anything he had said or done. No, it was only because she had condemned him for the deeds of the other men in her life. *I've been so stupid. I hope it's not too late. I'll make it up to him.*

Jeff said, "Let's go back up and check on Dad. It's getting late and I need to get home. I want to see how he's doing first."

"Would you mind giving me your phone numbers so I can contact you?" Carla pulled out a couple of business cards from her purse and handed one to each of them.

"Of course." Becky took a notepad out of her handbag and wrote down her number then handed it to Jeff so he could do the same.

Carla put the paper in her purse and followed them to Jason in ICU. She circled the hall slowly, shuffling her feet while the other two checked on Jason. They came out fifteen minutes later. She could tell by the looks on their faces the news wasn't good.

Carla looked up into Jeff's worried eyes. "How is he?"

Jeff's voice was somber, "Not good."

"The doctor said it's going to take time. Dad's condition is critical, but stable. They won't know any more until he wakes up." Becky touched Carla's wrist.

"Do they know when that might be?" Carla bit her lower lip, unaware of the pain.

Becky's face was downcast. "No. If they do, they aren't saying,"

Jeff gave his sister a hug. "I really have to get going. I'll come back in the morning. I wouldn't be much use at work tomorrow anyway. I know Cindy's worried. I want to go home and explain everything to her. I don't know what to tell my kids—they're too young to process all this—I'm having trouble handling it myself."

Becky said, "What about Gram and Gramps? They're waiting to hear something. What should I say?"

Jeff closed his eyes, tilted his head back. "Ohhh . . . I don't know . . . tell them the truth. Tell them we'll know more tomorrow."

"I'll call them when I get home." Becky readjusted the purse strap on her shoulder. "I need to leave. I won't say much to my family either. No need to worry them before we know anything. I'll just tell them that Grandpa is in the hospital for a while, but I won't say how serious it is. Ben is going to want to hear all the details. I'll stay home from work for a few days. They can get a substitute. I wouldn't be able to concentrate." She heaved a deep sigh.

Jeff asked. "Are you going to head home soon, Carla?"

"No. Think I'll just stay here. I want to be close by if anything happens. It's so far to go back home. I wouldn't be able to sleep anyway. I'll call my secretary and tell her to cancel my appointments for tomorrow. It's not the busiest time of year, so it will just take a little rearranging of my schedule. I'll have a neighbor feed my animals."

Becky thought of her Dad's farm, "I guess I'd better call Dad's neighbor and ask him to feed the horses."

"I already went over and took care of them. I gave each horse a bale of hay. They'll be all right for a couple of days. I gave the cats some extra food. They've been busy hunting, too."

"Thank you for doing that, but I'll still let Phil Thompson know that Dad has been hurt. He'll have to go over there sometime soon. I'll wait until tomorrow to call. I really must be going. I'm beat." Becky's shoulders sagged.

"Me too, I'll walk you down to the parking lot, Becky." Jeff gave Carla a hug. "You hang in there. I'm sure Dad's going to pull through."

Carla walked with them down the hall and waited with them for the elevator. She waved as the doors closed and they disappeared. She felt so alone once they were gone. Jeff and Becky seemed like such good people. Jason had done a good job raising them. It was obvious he was a very important part of their lives; that said something about his character. She hoped she would be lucky enough to share his life too.

She went down to the lobby, flopped into in an upholstered chair, and pulled out her cell phone. She called her neighbor Patti and explained the situation and asked her to take care of her animals. Then she called her mother.

As soon as she heard her mother's pick up, the tears came in a flood. "Oh . . . Mom."

"Carla . . . what's wrong? Where are you?"

"It's Jason . . . I'm at Harborview," she said with a sob.

"What about Jason? I thought you stopped seeing him."

Carla inhaled a deep breath, wiped her eyes with a tissue and blew her nose.

Her mother's voice was high pitched, the speech clipped, "Carla, are you there? What's happening?"

Carla exhaled loudly. Her voice came out in croaking spurts, "Jason . . . wa . . . was . . . in . . . a hor . . . horrible . . . accident." She sobbed.

"Oh . . . that's terrible. How is he? He wasn't killed?"

"No—but it's bad—real bad."

"What's his condition?"

"They won't know until he regains consciousness. He has a head injury." She blinked her eyes and blew her nose.

"Mom I've been so stupid."

"Carla, don't be hard on yourself."

"I met his son and daughter. They're really nice. I've been such an idiot."

"Honey, blaming yourself doesn't accomplish anything."

"I know."

"Think positive thoughts. I'll be praying for him. He'll get better."

"I hope you're right."

"Carla, don't dwell on your guilt. I'm sure he'll forgive you. Be strong. He's going to need you."

"You're right."

"Honey, take care of yourself."

'Thanks, Mom."

"You call me tomorrow."

"I will. Bye."

"Goodbye."

Carla took off her shoes, tucked her legs onto the chair, curled up and stretched her neck from side to side. She closed her eyes and rested her head on the chair-back. She dozed briefly then returned upstairs.

It was a long night. Nurses came in and out. Every time she inquired about his condition, she was given the same answer. There was no change.

The next morning she sat in the cafeteria sipping her coffee, staring at the unappetizing mass of scrambled eggs and dry sausage on the plate in front of her. She realized she could not hang out at the hospital indefinitely. Her own body would succumb to stress and lack of sleep and she would end up sick if she wasn't careful. She decided to make a hotel reservation for the night. She felt a little better knowing she'd be staying close by.

Carla deposited most of her breakfast into the trash and went to find a phone. She thumbed through the yellow pages in the phone book, selected a hotel and called to reserve a room. The price was exorbitant, but she would pamper herself. She could have gotten a cheaper place if she'd decided to stay farther away instead of downtown; on the other hand, she could have commuted from home.

She made a call to her office and asked Jasmine to cancel her appointments for the week. She didn't go into detail, just said a family emergency had come up.

Becky arrived early in the morning. Jeff showed up a couple of hours later. The two of them took turns sitting in the room with their dad and spending time with Carla.

The day passed with no change in Jason's condition. Becky and Jeff stayed until late afternoon then left Carla sitting alone in the hospital.

With her stamina wearing thin, Carla decided to check into the hotel. She stopped at a nearby store and purchased some new clothes. She hadn't thought to bring clothes when she left home. She had a light dinner, soaked in the hot tub, and went to bed early.

She spent a restless night trying to force visions of Jason, broken and in pain, lying in a hospital bed, out of her thoughts. Memories of pleasant times with him kept returning in guilt-ridden flashbacks. Aside from thoughts of Jason filling her mind, city noises played a role in keeping her awake. Honking horns and normal traffic sounds interrupted the quiet with irritating frequency. She was used to the stillness of country life and wondered how city dwellers could live with so much noise.

The next morning, clean and wearing fresh clothes, she was still exhausted. At least she felt a little bit more like herself. She went back to the hospital after breakfast. It was another long discouraging day spent pacing up and down the halls watching doctors, nurses and aides come and go. Jason's condition was unchanged. Jeff and Becky spent hours with her, but left in the late afternoon to care for their families. Carla promised to call them if there was any change in their dad's condition. She hung out until eight in the evening, then returned to her hotel room. It had been a depressing day. She called her neighbor, Patti, to make sure Garth, the horses and chickens were doing okay. Patti assured her they were doing fine and told her not to worry.

She castigated herself through much of the restless night. Memories of Jason haunted her thoughts. *Why couldn't I trust him? Why did I shut him out? I was such a fool.* Finally, she fell asleep only to wake up feeling tired in the morning. After a hurried breakfast, she returned to the hospital.

Becky was already there. She came out of Jason's room beaming. "Dad's conscious. The doctor sent me out so he can examine him."

"That's great news." Suddenly, Carla felt light-headed. A smile lit her eyes.

"He has a concussion, but they still don't know how serious it is. He's talking, but he doesn't remember what happened. I told him you were here. He didn't believe me." Becky winked at Carla.

"I spoke to the doctor and requested that they let you in to see him. He said the hospital doesn't let non-family members visit critically ill patients, but I convinced him it would be very beneficial for Dad to see you. He finally relented and said you can go in for a few minutes."

Carla was speechless. This was what she had been waiting for, but now that she would be seeing Jason, she suddenly panicked. *What will I say? What is he going to say? Will he forgive me?* Her knees felt weak and her hands trembled.

The doctor came out. "He isn't out of the woods yet. The concussion wasn't as serious as we'd originally feared. I was very concerned about swelling around the brain. For a while it looked like we might have to remove a section of his skull. Fortunately, that proved to be unnecessary. He should make a full recovery."

"Thank God!" Becky threw her arms around Carla.

Carla exhaled a deep breath, relieved and surprised by the younger woman's sudden display of affection.

The doctor gave them a minute to react to his words before continuing. "He has some rough times ahead. There are lots of bruises and contusions and some pretty deep lacerations besides the more serious injuries. He's looking at extensive recovery time and physical therapy once he heals well enough to progress to that step. He won't be running marathons anytime soon."

Becky had to tilt her head up to look the tall doctor in the eye. "My dad's a strong man, he'll get through this."

"We won't be moving him out of the ICU for a day or two. I want to keep him under observation until the swelling goes down and he's out of danger."

Carla couldn't keep the excitement out of her voice. "Can I see him?"

"Yes, but only for a few minutes. He needs quiet and rest for a few days."

"Thank you. I promise I won't be long." She opened the door and tentatively crossed the room to the bed.

Jason had casts on his right arm and leg. His torso and head were bandaged. His swollen face had numerous cuts and was badly bruised.

He turned his head and looked at her when she walked in. His raspy voice was barely audible, "My God, I must have died and gone to Heaven."

"Very funny."

"I'm not dead? I'm not dreaming? How else would I be looking at you?" He paused and sighed. "Are you really here? I thought I'd seen the last of you."

"It's me—in the flesh—I came as soon as I knew you were here. Actually, I came even before I knew for sure it was you."

His voice sounded sarcastic, "Really?"

She smiled. "Yes, really."

"How did you find out?"

"I recognized your truck on TV. At least I suspected it was you on the news." She explained what transpired since then, a brief synopsis. She didn't have much time.

His gravelly voice sounded a little hostile. "So—I had to come near death to see you?"

She looked at the IV line connected to his left wrist. He looked so pale.

She touched his arm. "I'm sorry."

"I wasn't going to hurt you. I don't understand why you couldn't believe that." He looked into her eyes.

"I realize that now."

His voice was weak. "What took you so long?" He tried to move his right casted arm and flinched in pain.

She admitted in a quiet voice, "I can't explain it."

"So I've heard before. Why do I have to keep paying a price for something that had nothing to do with me? What are you going to do now?"

She laid her fingers gently on his hand and stroked lightly. "I'll make it up to you. I promise."

"Forgive me if I find that hard to believe." He looked at her with narrow-slitted eyes sunken into puffy, blackened lids.

"I know my track record isn't very good. I haven't exactly done anything to earn your trust." She looked away, her eyes focused on the floor in the corner.

"Lady—that is a gross understatement," he growled.

She frowned. "You're not making this easy."

"*I'm* not making things easy? You've been a continuous uphill battle. One I've managed to keep losing, by the way." He pressed his lips together in a tight line.

She sighed. "I know—I'm *really* sorry about that."

"You're sorry?" His dull eyes pierced through her.

She paused before responding. "Yes."

"I already have too many broken body parts. I can't afford to have a broken heart on top of everything else."

"Don't worry, I won't do that. I'll prove it to you if you'll let me." She looked him straight in the eye.

"Tell me, why should I trust you? So far you're the one who's been untrustworthy."

It hadn't occurred to her he would be so unforgiving. "I guess I deserve this."

His voice softened a little, "Damn right you do."

"I'm just asking you to give me one last chance. I give you my word you won't regret it."

"I must be pretty stupid, or else just too brain damaged from my accident to use common sense and run the other way. Oh, wait a minute; I can't run anywhere, I'm a captive audience. You'll have your work cut out trying to prove I can trust you."

"You're being terribly difficult for someone who's supposed to be in pain."

"What do you mean *supposed to be*? Would you like to trade places?" He tried to sit up, pushing up with his good arm. He was too weak and the IV restricted his movement. "Unnhh." He gave up.

She couldn't stand to see him in so much pain. "You need to lie down—and no—I wouldn't want to be in your situation, but I didn't wish it on you either. I never wanted you to get hurt. I feel terrible about that.

I stayed here all night the first night you were here, briefly slept in the lobby, most of the time I was in the hall outside your door. I was very worried about you. I would give anything to undo what happened to you, but I can't." Tears rolled down her cheeks.

"You're wearing me out," he moaned.

"I'd better leave you alone now. I'll be right outside. I'll come back after you've had a chance to rest." She brushed her fingertips across his hand, then turned and left.

She sagged against the door and closed her eyes. Her chest heaved as a deep sigh escaped her lips.

Becky was waiting. She hurried over, wrapped her arm around Carla's shoulder and led her to a chair. "How did it go?"

"Ohhh . . . it was very hard to see him like that. I expected him to look hurt . . . but he looks worse than I imagined . . . the swelling . . .the bruises . . . He's so fragile. "She looked away for an instant." I don't think he was very happy to see me. He doesn't trust me." She shrugged her shoulders and took a deep breath. "I can't blame him. He seemed to forgive me though."

Becky gave her a hug. "Oh, I wouldn't worry about that. I'm sure he was thrilled to see you. His eyes lit up when I told him you were here."

Carla became serious. "I won't disappoint him."

Becky said, "I'm just going to peek in on him. I'll be right back." She opened the door and tip-toed in. Jason's eyes were closed and he was snoring. She slipped out and sat beside Carla. "He's sleeping."

Carla walked in and moved to Jason's good side on the left. He extended his arm and she grasped his hand. She was shocked by the feebleness of his condition. He had been so argumentative; she hadn't realized just how much his strength had been reduced. He was so fragile, she felt guilty for arguing with him earlier.

His tone had changed. "You *are* a sight for sore eyes. I am glad you're here."

"You are? You could have fooled me—are you sure?"

"Yes. I'm sure." He didn't sound very convincing.

"Am I forgiven?" She reached over and touched his cheek.

"That remains to be seen. Tentatively I would say so, but I'm putting you on probation." A ghost of a smile crossed his lips.

She breathed a sigh of relief. "I'm glad to hear that, I promise you won't regret it."

"I am going to hold you to that. Can I have a kiss?" He tried to reach for her but groaned with the effort.

She bent down and gave him a peck on the cheek.

"That wasn't exactly what I had in mind."

"You're in pain."

"My lips aren't broken."

"Are you sure? You look like you tried to stop a car with your face." She grinned, ran her finger across the chapped, cracked, and swollen lips that protruded from his beard and blackened, bruised and bloated face.

"I assure you they are in good working order. Yes, I want a better one," he insisted.

She leaned over and planted a long passionate kiss, on his lips.

"That was much better. More of those and I could be on the road to a much more rapid recovery." He smiled at her, his eyes taking on a new sparkle.

"I will do what I can to get you well." She gently stroked his hand.

"You're going to have me in a very bad way here if you keep that up."

"I guess I'll just have to stop then and we'll wait until you're recovered." She started to move away.

"Not yet, and I'll take a rain check on any further medical treatment, but I can handle this for a while." He pulled her back and gave her another long warm kiss. He was beginning to look better already.

She pulled away and said, "You need to get some rest, now. I'll come back later."

Carla leaned across the bed and adjusted the blanket around Jason's shoulder. He reached for her arm and pulled her towards him.

"I'd like a kiss."

"You're still swollen. You need to get better. I don't want to be responsible for hindering your healing," she teased with a smile.

"I don't need to be well first. This is the best therapy. Remember, it could be necessary for my complete recovery, not to mention my entire emotional well-being."

"Well then, we'll just have to make sure you participate in plenty of therapy." She squeezed his hand.

"I'll be counting on that." His expression changed to concern, "Who's feeding the animals?"

"Becky asked a neighbor, Phil Thompson, to do it. I fed them a lot before I came here. I went over to your place and gave each of your horses an extra bale of hay. "

"I'm sure they appreciated it."

She smiled and nodded her head. "They did.

"I fed the kittens. They're sure growing."

"Yes, they are. Thank you for doing that."

"You're welcome."

"Phil will take good care of them. He knows what to do."

The door opened and a nurse walked in. "I'm afraid you'll have to go now."

"All right, but I'm not leaving the hospital. I'll be right outside." Carla let go of his hand and started to leave.

His voice was gravelly. "Carla—"

"Yes." She stopped and looked at him.

"I'm glad you came." His smile glinted in his eyes in spite of black puffy lids.

"Me, too." She grasped the door knob. Her smile replaced concern on lips that could still feel the warmth of his.

She heard him ask the nurse. "When am I going to get out of here?" Carla went out and closed the door before she could hear the reply.

Every day, Carla was at the hospital. She observed and assisted when he went through physical therapy and learned how to transfer him to and from a wheelchair. It wasn't easy for either of them. He had good days and bad. Jason's recovery progressed at a slow but steady pace. He was impatient to go home.

After a week, the doctor was willing to release him from the hospital, but only if he had someone to take care of him.

Carla discussed the situation with his family. They decided it would be best if he stayed at Carla's house until he was well enough to be on his own. She could do much of her work from home, and she had no other family members living there to worry about. She volunteered to care for him during his convalescence.

Becky and Jeff were relieved she was willing to take on the responsibility, allowing them to return to their normal routines. Carla felt she owed it to Jason. It was the least she could do after the emotional ringer she'd put him through. She felt somewhat anxious about taking on the responsibility, but she was determined to see him through his recovery.

## Chapter 26

Jason sat on the edge of the bed while Carla and a nurse prepared him for his release from the hospital. He groaned and clenched his teeth as they maneuvered him into the wheelchair.

He exhaled. "Whew, I'll be glad when I get these casts off." Carla gathered his personal things, and checked to make sure she had everything.

"I'll pick you up at the entrance," she said, and hurried away to her car.

The nurse said, "You're doing well. A few more weeks and you'll be getting around much easier." She opened the door and rolled him down the hall. "We're going to miss you around here."

"I can't say I'll miss being in the hospital, but you've all taken very good care of me. I really appreciate everything you've done. Everyone was really nice," he said with a smile.

They waited out front for Carla to drive up. The nurse helped Carla transfer him in and fasten the seatbelt. She waved as they drove away.

Jason winced as the car bounced over the slight ridge at the edge of the driveway. "Uuuhhn." He gritted his teeth. "Watch the bumps."

"Sorry, I can't do much about that. I'll try to take it as easy as I can." She waited for a break in the traffic then headed for the freeway.

Traffic was congested in Seattle, typical even in the middle of the day. Once they left the city it was relatively light. South, in Federal Way, grooves in the pavement caused the car to shimmy. Carla looked over at Jason. His eyes were closed, fingers of his left hand pressed tight against the dashboard. His teeth bit into his lower lip. He sat silently until they pulled into the driveway an hour and a half later.

Carla got out and removed the wheelchair from the trunk. She rolled it to the passenger side and opened the door.

Garth sniffed the unfamiliar object. His nose gave the casts on Jason's arm and leg a once over before he turned his attention to the man. He wagged his tail and licked Jason's hand.

"Hi, boy, I know I don't look the same. You're going to have to get used to having me around. Think you can do that?"

Carla locked the brakes on the wheelchair. "Ready?"

"Ready as I'll ever be." Jason struggled to slide his butt out of the car as Carla reached over to help. He grimaced. "Ouch."

"Sorry." Carla was out of breath by the time she maneuvered him from the car and into the wheelchair. "I guess this is going to take practice."

She unlocked the brakes on the wheelchair and rolled him up the newly constructed ramp leading to her front door.

"You had this built for me?" Jason asked when he saw the ramp.

"Of course, it was nothing really."

In truth, it had been costly, but she never would have been able to get him in and out of the house without it.

It had taken Jason totally by surprise when she offered to take him into her home. At least something good had come out of this whole painful ordeal.

The ice queen had thawed. She never ceased to amaze him. Sometimes she acted like she didn't care at all; other times she was the most nurturing thoughtful person he'd ever known. He was optimistic this would be a positive step. He'd finally be with her, but too incapacitated to do anything about it. What rotten luck. He'd just have to make the best of it.

He was enraptured and confused by her. His heart was captured and couldn't break free and she pulled all the strings. As she rolled him into the house, he prayed this time would be different.

With broken ribs and only one usable arm and leg, there wasn't much Jason was able to do. The situation was made even worse since it was the right side that was damaged and he was right handed.

He was exhausted by the time she managed to get him settled into bed in the guest room. He hadn't complained, but she sensed his discomfort and saw the perspiration beading up on his brow.

"Can I have a glass of water, please? I think I better take a pain pill."

"Of course. I'll be right back."

She returned with a full glass and handed him a pill, then pulled up a chair to sit beside him.

He swallowed the pill. "Why the sudden change of heart? I'd all but given up on you, then I get hurt and there you are, a healing angel, just like you've been part of my life forever."

"I can't explain it. When I thought you were hurt it really affected me. Then when I met Jeff and Becky at the hospital—well—I realized I'd misjudged you.

He set the glass down and his fingers brushed softly across the top of her hand. "Possibly, but I don't think that's the whole picture. I think you care more about me than you care to admit to yourself."

She felt his penetrating eyes on her, piercing the last of her defenses. All those carefully contrived safeguards were gone, leaving her heart wide open, vulnerable. She knew before she invited him to stay that there'd be no retreat. She crossed a bridge and there was no turning back. Perhaps she'd live to regret it, but after getting to know his family, the risk seemed small. She wanted to get to know him better.

Carla held his hand as he drifted off to sleep, then she tiptoed out of the room and went to the barn to feed the horses. She'd brought both of Jason's horses over a couple of days after he regained consciousness. Even the cats were moved into her barn. The horses whinnied, eager to be fed. She tossed in hay and scooped grain into the feeders. A cat rubbed against her leg as she poured cat food into a dish. He purred as she rubbed his head. "I better get you guys neutered soon. We certainly don't need any more of you."

She walked by her garden on the way back to the house and looked with disgust at the overgrown weeds. Spending so much time in Seattle took a toll on her yard work. She needed to get dinner started. It would be nice to have home-cooked meals again.

Ravenous, and sick of hospital food, Jason awoke to the aroma of roasting meat. Carla came in with a steaming tray.

"That looks great." He tried to sit up higher.

"Thank you." She set up another tray near the bed so they could have their meal together. "Here, let me help you." She propped him up and adjusted the pillows behind his back.

"That's better." He reached for her with his good arm. She smiled and caressed his fingers. She straightened out his covers.

She had taken the time to cut everything into bite size pieces so he wouldn't have to struggle with one arm. He ate every bite, savoring each mouthful. He felt better already after the delicious meal and her caring hands.

She cleared the trays and disappeared into the kitchen. Garth stayed with him, laying his head on the bed. Jason stroked the top of the canine head and massaged behind his ears.

"Sorry, boy, I can't do a very good job until I get my arm back in shape."

Carla walked back into the room. "I see my faithful companion is very fickle."

"He's an excellent judge of character."

"Is he?" Her lips curved into a crooked grin.

"Yes. Come over here and keep me company." He patted the side of the bed next to him. "You don't have to worry. With one leg and one arm, I'm rendered harmless."

A smile lit up her face as she sat down on the bed beside him. His attention turned from the dog and he reached over and touched her hand.

"I may only have one arm for the time being, but I'm not entirely useless." He failed to suppress a groan as he struggled to shift his position in her direction.

"Be careful. You don't want to hurt yourself." Her voice sounded concerned.

"I'll be careful; anyway, you're worth a little pain." He pulled her over to him and gave her a long penetrating kiss. "Mmmmm . . . that was good."

"Yes, it was," she admitted, her arms wrapped around him, her fingers massaging the muscles of his shoulder and neck.

"I'm feeling much better already. You are the best kind of physical therapy."

"This isn't helping your broken body parts."

"No, but part of me can still function pretty well without them."

He kissed her on the mouth again. His hand caressed her neck then lowered down to brush across her breasts. He felt her nipples harden beneath her shirt. She kissed him back, her arms wrapping around his neck, carefully avoiding putting pressure on his injured arm and ribs. He kissed her throat, felt her throbbing pulse, and moved lower down the front of her shirt. He slid his hand beneath the fabric and cupped her gently in his hand.

Carla moaned.

Encouraged, he asked in a husky voice, "Can I unbutton your shirt?"

"Yes, I don't mind."

Using only one hand, he fumbled with the first button.

Carla unbuttoned the rest and unfastened her bra for him. His attention focused first on one firm breast and then the other, the palm of his hand brushing and kneading the tender aureole, eliciting a response that hardened the tips. His warm lips surrounded her sensitive nipples, sucking and kissing, while his fingers worked gently, caressing her heated skin. He returned to those warm full lips and kissed her; she returned his overtures with increasing enthusiasm.

Heat coursed through her in waves as her body welcomed his advances. Release of pent up desire overwhelmed her to the depths of her core. Her greedy hands clutched him as she felt herself giving in, responding.

He knew he could manage somehow, but wanted to wait until he knew she was ready.

He wanted her to need him, to crave him with that same fiery passion he felt for her. He yearned to fill her and bring her to ecstasy, to satisfy her desire and feel her heat. He knew he could do it, but not now. He wanted her to choose him, at her own time, with no regret. His hardened flesh was at odds with his mental constraint, his own needs unmet, he pulled back determined to wait.

A puzzled look crossed her face as he retreated. Confused, she stared into the deep pools of his eyes. "Am I hurting you?"

"Oh no, it's not that." He hadn't thought she would attribute his hesitation to his current physical condition. "It's still too soon. I want to be sure you're ready. I don't want you to have any second thoughts."

"Okay." She didn't disagree. With all the times she'd rejected him in the past, she knew he was probably leery of her intentions. *Am I ready?* She thought so, but perhaps he was right. The dampness of her flaming skin left her feeling regret that he had stopped.

She knew he desired her, she could feel the hardness of his erection. That he was willing to forego his own pleasure was proof of the degree to which he was prepared to protect her feelings. She was moved by his thoughtful sincerity.

She rose from the bed and gave him a kiss. "Do you need anything else tonight?" She pulled her shirt around her and buttoned her blouse.

"Would you help me get into the bathroom?"

"Of course."

They accomplished that task with some degree of difficulty. Once he was back in bed, she set a urinal on the nightstand by the bed along with a bottle of water.

She tucked the covers around him. "Anything else?"

He laughed. "You aren't going to get up if I want something in the middle of the night."

"I will if you have an emergency. Yell if you need anything. I'm a light sleeper."

"I'll be fine, thanks."

"See you in the morning. Goodnight."

"Goodnight."

She retreated to her room, but sleep was a long time coming. She couldn't stop thinking of him just down the hall. She could feel his hands on her, gentle, sensuous. Her body hungered for him. She fought to put the images aside, until at long last, sleep came, but he invaded her dreams.

In the morning, she entered his room. "Good morning. How are you today?"

"Just wonderful, not everything about this ordeal is bad. After all, I have the pleasure of being your captive. How else could I have accomplished that?"

She playfully punched him lightly on the shoulder. "Very funny. Would you like to wash up?"

"I would, but it's a little difficult with only one hand, especially since I can't get one leg, my chest or my right arm wet."

"I know, that's why I'm going to help you."

"Oh—really. In that case, I would like to get cleaned up."

"That's good because it's not optional. You stink."

"Sorry, I haven't been able to take a shower."

"First you're going to have a sponge bath, then I'm going to wash your hair."

"All of me? That sounds like fun. I'm looking forward to it already."

"Well, most of you. You do still have one good arm after all."

He threw his covers aside. She helped him into the wheelchair and rolled him into the bathroom. A clean set of underwear, brand new pair of shorts, and navy blue button down short sleeve shirt were waiting.

She'd done some shopping for him, making some purchases that would be easy to get on.

Carla helped him out of his clothes, covered the casts with plastic, then transferred him to the shower chair. She placed a washcloth and towel within his reach and tested the water temperature. She handed him the showerhead. "Let me know when you need help."

He was in there for a while before he finally called her. "I'm ready for anything now." He winked and flashed a teasing smile.

She lathered soap onto the washcloth and carefully raised his right hand. His teeth clenched so she knew it was painful, but he'd given no other indication he was uncomfortable.

"Make sure you get my armpits."

"Don't worry."

She couldn't help but notice he was in good shape in spite of the accident. Soap swirled through the hairs above his chest and she lingered there longer than necessary cleaning as much as she could above and below his taped ribs.

"Do you want to do the rest yourself?" She was hesitant to scrub his private parts before she had even had any contact with them.

"You're doing just fine. I trust you to take good care of me."

She soaped up his genitals and felt his erection beneath her hands.

"I told you I was ready for anything." He grinned.

Embarrassed, she finished quickly, then rinsed him off. She dried him with a soft, fluffy towel and helped him get dressed.

He'd made no attempt to lure her into a physical dalliance even though his own desire was blatant. His patience was a difficult challenge, but he was determined to have her come to him.

She wheeled him to the kitchen table. They chatted over breakfast and he noticed her eyes roving over his body. He said nothing about it, allowed her to think about him. He hoped she was starting to think of him as often as he thought about her.

She settled Jason on the sofa, handed him the remote and brought in some books and a newspaper in case he felt like reading. Garth lay at his feet.

"I need to take care of the animals so I'll be out for a while. Do you need anything before I go?"

"I'll be fine."

She pulled on her coat and opened the door. Normally, Garth would have bounded out ahead of her. Instead, his eyes followed her, but he didn't move.

The horses greeted her as usual. "I haven't seen you much lately. That's going to change."

She ran her hands over Shazan as he ate his grain. "I need to work with you a lot more than I have been," she crooned. "Now that Jason is out of the hospital, I'll be able to concentrate on your training again."

Ever since the accident, her world had been turned upside down. She realized she had led a mundane existence before all this. She was growing accustomed to having Jason in her life. Her body was reacting to him in ways she was finding more and more difficult to suppress. Thoughts of him kept her awake at night.

She could feel his lips, tongue and hands touching her all over. Erotic fantasies crept into her thoughts and fired up her body with desire. She craved him with all of her being. It was impossible to push thoughts of him from her mind. Her impenetrable walls of defense had been broken down and destroyed. There was no turning back.

## Chapter 27

Today was the day. Jason had waited eight long weeks. The casts were finally coming off. Granted, it hadn't all been bad. He was convinced Carla might have resisted him forever without the catalyst of the mudslide. Confident he was part of her life now, he was eager to move ahead with their relationship.

He was anxious to get back to work. He hadn't even been in his own house since the accident. They had driven by a few times on the way back from the hospital and the clinic, but he couldn't get up the steps to go inside.

Carla rolled him into the doctor's office and waited outside. Sometime later, he walked out. He had a pronounced limp and used a cane. It would take some time to be back to normal. By the smile on his face, she knew things would only get better.

"Shall we go home?" He couldn't contain his enthusiasm. He felt wonderful, lighter, unencumbered by the troublesome casts, able to scratch his skin when it itched.

Carla had mixed emotions about his recovery. She was pleased he would be able to get around on his own again. It had been quite a drain on her energy and time to take care of him in addition to the usual chores of running the farm and her business, but she was accustomed to having him around now.

It would leave a gap in her life when he moved out. She was unsure how she would feel in her house once he was actually gone.

\* \* \*

Carla loaded his things into her car. Silence prevailed as they drove to his house. He managed to work his way up the steps and unlock the door. She followed him inside and he flipped on the light. It was chilly and a faint musty odor was evident, the result of having the heat turned down for so long. Other than that, it was just as he left it.

"I'll bring everything in." She turned and walked out, and returned carrying a bag of groceries. Once all his food, clothes and toilet articles were put away, she told him, "Well, I guess I better leave. I've got a lot to do and you probably do too."

"Oh." He hadn't really thought about what life would be like back in his own house.

She gave him a kiss goodbye and turned to leave. With a sad empty feeling, he watched her drive away.

He'd gotten used to being part of her life and seeing her every day. The thought of being back in his house alone filled him with longing already.

He ambled outside and worked his way down the back steps to the porch swing and sat down. Memories of the last time he sat there, so many months ago with Carla, came flooding back. Much had changed since then.

He walked out to the gazebo to check on the hot tub. The water was cool to the touch. He turned up the thermostat. He planned on spending a lot of time in there now that he could get his leg and arm wet. The doctor had told him that soaking in hot water would be good therapy and he could exercise his damaged limbs. It would help speed his recovery.

Back inside, everything was in place and he sat in front of the TV, but he didn't see what was on the tube. Somehow, his house no longer felt like home. There was a great void in his life now. He had only been home a few hours, but he missed Carla.

Carla fed the horses and cats . She had decided it would be better to leave Jason's animals with her until he was in a little better shape. She didn't mind keeping them for a while. They were all getting along; besides, now that Jason was gone she would have more time. She walked past the chickens. They followed her along the wire and clucked loudly as she walked away.

She started back to the house. Garth had his nose to the ground, following the scent of some animal no doubt. He looked up to see she was almost to the steps. Ending his pursuit, he ran full-bore to catch up to her.

"Well, come on. Let's go in."

Wagging his tail, tongue lolling out, he followed her up the steps.

She prepared dinner and sat down to eat. Normally, she enjoyed her meals, but it seemed tasteless this evening. She looked at Garth lying on his bed in the corner. He was busy chewing a rawhide bone; the soggy, gnarled leather succumbed to his substantial teeth.

She should have been content, the extra burden of caring for Jason no longer a pressure. Relief was curiously absent. She cleaned up the dishes, and then sat on the sofa. She picked up a magazine, flipped through the pages, closed it, stared into space.

Life should be getting back to normal, but what was normal? Jason had affected her so much. She couldn't stop thinking about him. She missed his acerbic sense of humor and the brilliant smile that so often lit his face. She could visualize him in her mind's eye, and his absence was somehow unnerving. Well, he just left. It would take time to readjust. She put the magazine down.

Carla picked up the phone and speed dialed. "Hello Mom."

"Hello, I'm so glad you called. I've been thinking about you."

Carla's voice was flat, "Jason moved back home today."

"Ohhh—no wonder you sound so down in the dumps. Sounds like you've grown pretty fond of Jason."

Carla smiled. "Yes, I guess I have."

"I'm glad to hear that. I can hardly wait to meet the man who finally managed to thaw your frozen heart. Practically killed him to do it."

Carla laughed. "Mom—you're starting to sound like Jason."

"Good, I'm sure I'll like him."

"Yes, you will, and I know he'll like you."

"You're sounding more cheerful. Yes, I'm feeling better, now."

"Good, glad I could help. I'm going to go to bed now. Call again soon, or better yet, come by and see me."

"I will. Talk to you soon Mom."

"Bye."

Carla sat there in silence for a while after she hung up the phone. Several minutes later she decided to call it a night and went to bed. If she started work early that should help take her mind off him. But sleep was a long time coming.

The next day, work seemed to drag endlessly. Her thoughts kept returning to Jason. It was difficult to stay focused. Finally, the long day came to an end.

Her voice sounded more cheerful than she felt. "Jasmine, have a nice evening."

"You too, Carla, see you tomorrow."

Carla decided to go riding after work. It had been ages since she'd been on the back of a horse. Rainy weather had been a deterrent, plus all the extra time spent caring for Jason had consumed most of her time. She would make up for that now.

Soon she was astride Angel, cantering along the familiar path, cool air tousling her hair. The rhythmic gait of her well-muscled mount filled her heart with insurmountable joy.

The call of a bald eagle caught her attention and she watched the great bird circle above until it disappeared behind a stand of tall fir. Solitude and serenity blended with the evergreen scented air, providing the environment she enjoyed so much. This day was really no different. The familiar components were all there, but something was missing—Jason. She just couldn't get him out of her mind and heart. Finishing her ride, she returned home, wishing he'd be there to greet her.

Back in the barn, she unsaddled Angel, brushed the mare down and turned her free. Everyone fed; she walked back to the house and slipped off her riding boots.

The phone rang. She noticed the caller ID. Her face lit up in a smile. "Hello, Jason."

"Good evening."

The familiar masculine voice caused her heart to beat faster.

"What are you doing?"

"I just came back from riding. I'm not doing anything at the moment."

"Good. How about coming over and getting into the hot tub with me? I'm supposed to be doing it for therapy, you know."

"That does sound nice. I haven't ridden for so long, I'm a little sore."

"Well then, it sounds like you could use some therapy, too."

She could feel his smile through the phone line. "Let me get cleaned up and I'll be right over." The words were out of her mouth before she even thought about hesitating.

It was only after she hung up that the reality of what she had committed herself to set in. She would go there and be with him. No more fantasizing about what it would be like.

She drove over to his house and ascended the steps. He met her at the door, wearing a navy blue robe.

He gave her a hug and a brief kiss. "Hi, are you ready to go down to the hot tub?"

"Sure." She tried to sound more confident then she felt.

"Would you mind carrying these for us?" He gestured to a pair of wineglasses and a bottle of wine sitting on the table.

"I can do that." She followed him out the back door.

"Sorry, I'm not much help. I still have a ways to go."

"You don't need to apologize. No one knows better than I do what you went through. I think you are doing quite well."

"All thanks to you." He made his way up the steps into the gazebo. "You can set those down." He gestured to the small table next to the tub.

He struggled to open the wine.

"Here, let me do that." She took the bottle, uncorked it and filled their glasses.

"Guess I'm still partially disabled." He set the timer on the water jets, slipped out of his robe and couldn't stifle the grimace of pain as he climbed into the hot bubbling water.

She handed him a glass, and then stripped out of her sweats. She pulled a hair clip out of the pocket of her sweatshirt, twisted her and pinned it up.

His eyes roamed over her body with appreciation. "You're so beautiful."

"Thank you." She felt herself blush. He had never seen her naked before.

She finished her wine and refilled her glass. "Are you ready for more?"

"No, thank you. I'm fine." He figured she needed it more than he did.

Carla felt more relaxed now, and came closer to him. He reached out a hand to her and she put her hand in his. She snuggled up to him, enfolded him in her arms and kissed his lips.

"Well, this is progress." He searched her eyes. "Do you trust me at last?"

"I guess I'm ready to find out."

"You won't be sorry." His arms tightened around her and his tongue flicked inside her mouth, sweet with the taste of wine.

She returned his kiss, ran her hands down his chest, over his thighs until she was grasping the muscles of his buttocks. Soft kisses brushed his chest as his hands circled her sensitive breasts, first one, then the other; he gave each one equal attention.

His lips found a hardened nipple and he sucked gently. Hands and lips explored and pleasured her. His erection pressed hard against her leg. She stroked him, her velvet fingers pleasuring him in return.

His tongue explored her mouth as his arms wrapped around her. She clung to him, her fingers clasping the firm muscles of his back. She was careful not to press too hard on his injured arm or ribs. A sudden pang of fear alarmed her. "Am I hurting you?"

"No, I'm fine," he panted, pulled her closer. His fingers explored the insides of her thighs, stroked her sensitive skin. She moaned with pleasure. He entered her and her body welcomed him. Her arms encircled him, pulling him tighter against her. His lips found hers and the kissed with passion.

Carla pressed her hands against his buttocks, pulled him deeper inside. Her heart pounded as they surged together, their energy churning the heated water long after the jets had stopped. Breathless and happy, they clasped each other, spent and hot.

"I'm roasting." Carla released herself from his embrace, pulled herself up out of the water and sat on the rim of the tub. He sat next to her with his arms around her waist and gave her a warm wet kiss. "Any regrets?"

"No." In fact her only regret at the moment was that she had put him off for so long. She felt alive—marvelous. He was so much more than she could have hoped.

"Does that mean we can do this again?" He kissed her cheek.

"Yes." She smiled. "I'd like that."

"I've finally found acceptance with the formerly unattainable Carla Summers."

She laughed. "Yes, you have. I'm sorry it took so long." She pulled him towards her till their lips met again.

"I'm glad you finally came to your senses and recognized a good man when you found one." He climbed out and kissed her and wrapped her in a large towel. "Here, you better get dried off before you catch a cold."

"I'm not cold yet." She dried herself off, let her hair down and then slipped into her clothes.

He was covered up, wrapped in his robe. She threw her arms around him and kissed him again, reluctant to let him go.

## Chapter 28

Greg Collier had already been convicted of the murders of Tim Sutton and Janice Williams. Another jury was given the task of determining the penalty phase: Life or Death.

Nervous family members had vented their emotions and desires to the defendant as well as the jury and, one by one, teary-eyed, angry and embittered, each expressed rage and sadness over the unthinkable loss.

It was the only chance to have some input to the court. No longer bystanders subjected to the emotional pain the testimony elicited, they could let the jury know the void that filled their lives due to the cruel defendant seated before them. The permanence of his acts could not be undone. Now, they wanted to exact the same punishment on him that he forced on their loved ones.

The final speaker, Greg Collier's mother, Nora, slumped in her wheel chair, and brushed tears from her eyes as she gave an impassioned plea for leniency to spare the life of her only son. She was loyal to the life she had created, nurtured and loved. She felt sorrow for the families he had victimized, but that did not lessen her own grief.

Most of the jurors wiped tears from their eyes as they listened to her heartfelt pleas. They struggled to maintain their composure. There were no winners here. The burden being placed on them was a difficult one to bear. One by one, they filed out to begin the process of deliberation.

Reporters stood outside the courthouse. Janice Williams' parents and sister stepped up to a mike.

Her mother leaned against her husband for support. "I feel no sympathy for Mr. Collier. He is a brutal sociopath. He gave no quarter to our daughter. I want none for him." She moved away followed by her family members.

Tim Sutton's brother spoke next, short and brief. "I want that son-of-a-bitch to die. One way or another, he's headed to hell."

\* \* \*

Renfield and Chandry hurried into the courthouse, avoiding numerous members of the news media as they entered the courtroom. It wouldn't be long now. Once the call came that the jury had reached a verdict, they came straight over. They sat in the packed room, anxious, expectant.

Members of the jury were brought in. Several of them displayed obvious signs of stress. The foreman handed the results to the bailiff who passed it on to the judge, who glanced at the form in silence and asked the foreman for the jury's verdict.

"We recommend the defendant be given life in prison without possibility of parole, Your Honor."

"Thank God." Collier's mother blurted.

Janice William's mother and sister broke into sobs. The defendant sat unmoving; no emotion discernible on the hardened features of his face; cold gray eyes devoid of tears stared straight ahead. Then slowly, almost imperceptibly, his cruel mouth hinted at a smile.

\* \* \*

Jason sat on the sofa, Garth lay at his feet. He turned on the evening news while Carla worked on dinner in the kitchen.

The newscaster announced, "Today, a Kitsap County jury has sentenced convicted killer, Greg Collier, to life in prison without the possibility of parole."

Jason called out. "Carla, Greg Collier was sentenced to life in prison today!"

She walked in and turned her attention to the TV. "He should have gotten the death penalty. The jurors must have felt sorry for his mother." They listened as family members reacted to the decision.

"At least that's over," Carla said. "Those people will never get over what he did, but hopefully they'll get some satisfaction knowing he will never be free for the rest of his life. He will rot in prison and die there."

"I hope so, but it affected me, and I barely knew the victims." Jason still dealt with his own memories of the crime; vivid images that reappeared without warning.

The newscaster turned to the next topic. "A multiple car fatality accident on I-90 near Issaquah . . ."

Carla went back to the kitchen.

After dinner, she sat down beside him. "I signed us up for water aerobics."

"Water aerobics? I don't have time for that."

"Neither do I, but I believe it's important for your recovery."

"I don't know . . ."

"We'll do it together. It'll be fun."

He looked skeptical. "I guess I can give it a try."

She touched his cheek and ran her fingers across the soft hair of his beard. "Good. You need the exercise. It'll be easier in the water."

He let out an exasperated sigh. "When do we start?"

"Tomorrow; we need to be in the pool by eight-thirty in the morning."

"What about work? I need to start before then."

"You aren't working full time yet and this will help you recover faster."

She cuddled up to him and kissed his cheek. "I've got to get home. I'll pick you up at quarter to eight. Wear your swimsuit and bring a towel and change of clothes."

"All right, as long as you're going with me. I guess I should do something to get my body in better shape." He stretched his right leg and gingerly rubbed the thigh muscle.

"Good, now I've got to go. I'll see you in the morning."

"I'll be ready." He heard the door close and listened as she drove down the driveway.

* * *

The next morning Carla finished her chores, ate a light breakfast, and grabbed her shoulder bag with a hairbrush, clean underwear, water shoes, towel, shampoo, conditioner, wash cloth, deodorant and soap. "Time to pick up Jason," she told Garth.

The dog whined in response. She left him outside and set her bag and purse in the car. A half hour later she and Jason pulled into the parking lot at the community club in Port Orchard.

Carla came out from the dressing room first. It took Jason longer to get out of his street clothes. He limped to the edge of the pool where she stood waiting. Several ladies were in the water ahead of them.

"Are you ready to get in?" Carla asked.

"I guess." He grabbed onto the railing, looked at his jagged scars, and slowly worked his way down the steps. Warm and inviting, the water felt good against his injured leg.

Carla followed him and they moved into deeper water. Two women moved apart to make room for them.

Music started and the instructor, Gail, demonstrated stretching exercises to start them off. After a few minutes, the real workout began. The pace picked up and they were all lifting arms and legs, churning the water.

"Rocking horse, one leg forward, one leg back, don't change legs," Gail announced.

Jason was doing pretty well on his left leg, but when the command came to change legs, he felt the pain from his injury. *I'm really out of shape.* He noticed that not everyone kept pace or moved their arms as much. Water splashed and small waves rippled around pumping bodies.

Carla took deep breaths, in through her nose out through her mouth. Her legs were beginning to ache. She looked over at Jason. His face was red and he was grimacing in pain. He slowed down and took deep breaths.

"Jog, swing your arms! One minute. Five, four, three, two, one. Breath in through your nose, arms up. Hold your breath. Breathe out through your mouth. Arms down.

*Thank God she slowed down.* Jason rubbed his aching leg.

"Move against the side of the pool—runner's stretch." Gail demonstrated.

"See you all tomorrow."

Jason groaned.

"How'd you do?" Gail asked him.

"I'm a bit sore. My body hasn't recovered from an accident yet."

"Just do what you can. Don't push yourself too hard. Not everyone in here can do everything and it gets easier."

"I hope so. "This was harder than I thought it would be."

"We'll be back tomorrow," Carla said.

* * *

The next day Carla and Jason got to the pool early.

Jason slid into the water, "My legs are killing me. I'm taking it easier today."

By the time the hour was over, Jason was sure he had worked muscles he hadn't used in years.

He looked at Carla. She was laughing and talking to a bulky woman, whose knees bore the telltale scars of knee replacement. In fact, he had noticed quite a few of the other members of the group were visibly scarred. *I fit right in.*

He had to admit that even though he hadn't really wanted to be here, it was helping him already. He was in pain, but it was good pain, if there was such a thing. He was grateful to Carla for bringing him.

## Chapter 29

Carla worked Shazan on a lunge line in the corral. The colt's training was coming along very well, his gait changes smooth, responses immediate. He held his head high and his tail up, flowing behind the sleek black body.

Jason leaned on the fence, impressed by the quality of the animal as well as with Carla's training ability. Every time he looked at her, he was overjoyed that she'd finally welcomed him into her life.

She turned the horse loose and walked over to him, dimples accentuating the brilliant smile radiating across her face. "He's making great progress, isn't he?"

"Yes, he's an impressive animal. You're doing wonders with him. He's progressing better than I expected."

"Oh, you don't have confidence in me?"

"Of course, I do. You know that's *not* what I meant."

"I know." She laughed. "What do you say we go riding? Are you up to it?"

Jason hadn't ridden since the disaster. He was feeling reasonably good now, even though he still had a slight limp. Water aerobics had been a great help in speeding up his recovery. "Yes, I'd like to go." He rubbed his leg. "I think I can handle it."

"We'll just take it slow and go for a short ride. I don't think we should go too far. You're still not a hundred per cent.

"But I'm doing pretty well."

"I'll get the horses ready." She rolled up the lunge line and walked into the barn.

Soon they rode into the tree farm. A slight breeze rustled through the trees. The raucous call of a Steller's jay betrayed his location, brilliant blue plumage visible, as he shifted from tree to tree.

They left him behind and made their way along the winding dirt road. An amber sun peeked out from behind one of the many fluffy clouds that dotted the pale blue sky. The scent of wild roses accentuated the evergreen permeated aroma. It was a marvelous day with no rain in sight.

Garth ran ahead, hot on the trail of a red Douglas squirrel. Scolding chatter erupted from the side of a tree as it made its escape.

They reached the knoll and Jason turned in the saddle. "Shall we stop here?"

"Sounds good to me." Carla dismounted and tied her horse to a tree.

He sat down beside her on the log, removed his dark cowboy hat and scratched the top of his head. He set his hat down beside him, embraced her and gave her a kiss. He was overcome with emotion as she returned his overture with equal fervor.

"Just a minute." He stood up. Taking her hand, he led her to a clearing between two rows of trees. He removed his jacket and laid it on the ground. Lying down, he pulled her down beside him and wrapped her in his arms. Her warm lips met his, all else in the world forgotten, as they allowed themselves to be consumed by their shared passion.

"I like these snaps." Jason had no trouble unfastening Carla's new western shirt. Soon, her breasts lay exposed to his lips and hands as he tasted first one, and then the other.

Her hands clutched him, finding their way beneath his clothes. She kneaded the muscles in his back; her fingernails trailed delicately down to his buttocks. He kissed her. His fingers ran through her hair and caressed her neck. He buried his face in the cleft between her breasts, his silky beard brushing her softly. Her warm skin tingled beneath his gentle touch as his hands caressed her inner thighs and teased her sensitive nerves. Waves of pleasure surged through her needy body as she pulled him into her. They reached pinnacles of pleasure, there in the open on a bed of wild flowers. Satiated, they lay exhausted, entwined, content, fulfilled.

"Carla, I love you," he whispered, brushing the tip of a finger across her cheek.

"I love you too." Her lips found his. They kissed tenderly in a warm embrace.

He summoned up his nerve. "Will you marry me?" It hadn't been easy to come up with the courage to ask in spite of the fact that he'd been wanting to for some time.

"Are you sure you want to? Maybe we should just live together."

"Carla, I don't want to just live with you. I want you to be my wife. I want you to be with me for the rest of my life."

She wasn't prepared for his question. Even though it caught her by surprise, she couldn't deny she'd thought of it herself. Once determined never to marry again, now that the possibility presented itself, was it still so offensive? She had to admit it was not.

She loved Jason with all her heart. He's everything she ever desired in a man. She couldn't imagine her life without him. "Yes. I'll marry you."

His arms tightened around her and he kissed her on the lips, neck and throat. Enraptured, they found passion again.

She giggled. "What if someone comes by and sees us here?"

"It's a little late to worry about that now," he grinned, "but we should be heading back." His arm and leg still ached and even though they had not made a long ride, and the added physical exertion of their romantic interlude added to his discomfort. He was anxious to get home and take it easy for a while. They dressed and remounted.

Jason wasn't up to a bone-jarring trot and even a smooth canter was more than he could take after the ride out and their love making. Carla was content to pass the time at a leisurely pace as they plodded along. The methodical clip-clopping of hooves was interrupted occasionally by a snorting horse.

Pulling up at the pond, Jason wanted to stop. He dismounted and handed the reins to Carla, plucked some wildflowers, purple selfheal and red clover, tossed them into the dark water. He still felt sadness over the senseless brutality of the crime. He prayed the victims were at peace. He took the reins and remounted his horse and they moved on.

Back at the barn, they dismounted and Carla noticed Jason wincing in pain. Perhaps it had been too soon for him to go riding. His limp was much more pronounced than before they had left.

"I'll take care of the horses. You go on into the house and relax for a while." She took the reins from his hand.

"Thank you. I'm sorry I'm not up to helping you. Guess I'm not in as of good shape as I thought I was. I need to put my leg up for a while." He limped away, Garth at his side.

Carla finished with the horses and walked back to the house. Jason lay asleep on the sofa. He looked so peaceful; she didn't want to disturb him.

He awoke some time later to tantalizing aromas coming from the kitchen. His growling stomach reminded him how hungry he was.

Carla walked in, noticed he was awake. "How are you feeling?"

"I'm a little sore and my leg is stiff. I'll be okay."

"Dinner's almost ready, nothing fancy, stroganoff and a tossed salad."

"Mmmm, it sure smells good." He always looked forward to eating anything she cooked.

After a quiet dinner, they sat together on the sofa, relaxed and comfortable. Time and Jason's injury had permitted them to develop a closeness that just felt right.

"How about a massage for your leg?" Carla offered.

"That would be wonderful." Jason stood and walked into her bedroom, removed his jeans and stretched out on the bed. Carla bent down and gently kneaded his injured leg, rubbing massage oil into his aching muscles.

He closed his eyes, relaxed and allowed the pain to dissipate.

"Where are we going to live?" Carla had been hesitant to ask. "I would like you to come here. I have more room. Besides, your animals are already here."

"I can fix up my house and rent it out."

"I'll help you. We can work on it together."

"Come here." He pulled her down and gave her a long kiss.

Her heart was his.

# Chapter 30

"I'm sure glad that's done." Carla wiped an arm across her face, smeared paint across her sweaty brow.

"Me too. I think you've got almost as much paint on you as you put on the house." Jason laughed as he stepped down off the ladder.

"You're one to talk. You've got at least as much paint on you as I do." Carla couldn't hold back her own laughter at the sight of his paint-spattered beard. "It's a good thing we decided to paint it brown. At least you're color coordinated." She ran a finger across a blob of paint on his nose.

"Ha—ha, very funny." He looked down at his spotted overalls.

She set down her brush. "Well, let's get cleaned up and go home. I'm looking forward to a long, soak in the hot tub. I'm sure glad we had the Gazebo moved to my place."

"*Our* place," he corrected.

They hosed off their painting supplies, washed up and changed out of their paint-spattered clothes.

They stood outside to admire their work. The fence repaired and newly painted, framed the yard nicely. The grass was clipped and flowers bloomed in beds around the house. Everything looked picture perfect.

Jason looked at Carla and was overcome with love for this woman, his wife. He threw his arms around her and lifted her off the ground. She laughed and kicked her feet as he spun her around.

"What do you think, Mrs. Gerard? Shall we go home and spend some time in the hot tub?"

"That sounds like a good plan, Mr. Gerard. Let's go!"

He set her back down and they shared a long passionate kiss before he locked up the house. He drove out of the driveway, past the FOR RENT sign, and they headed home.

# About the Author

**Karen Lovett** graduated from the University of Washington with a Bachelor of Science degree in Zoology. She was a research technologist at Fred Hutchinson Cancer Research Center until she moved to the island of Okinawa, Japan where she studied fashion design. She has traveled extensively throughout Asia. has spent time in England, France, Holland and Scotland.

An all-breed rabbit judge with the American Rabbit Breeders Association, she has judged rabbit shows throughout the United States and Canada.

She plays guitar and enjoys writing poetry, songs, walking in the woods, gathering wild mushrooms with other members of the Kitsap Peninsula Mycological Society, swimming, water aerobics, or spending time at the beach. She maintains her rabbitry, gardens and orchard on a small farm on the Key Peninsula.

She is a staff writer for the *Key Peninsula News* and a member of two writers groups on the Key Peninsula. She hunts mushrooms in the forests near the farm she maintains, writes poetry and songs. She is currently working on her second novel.

CPSIA information can be obtained at www.ICGtesting.com
Printed in the USA
BVOW070732260412

288668BV00001B/1/P